A natural history of
of
Owls

A natural history of
Owls

Michael Everett

Hamlyn
London · New York · Sydney · Toronto

Published by The Hamlyn Publishing Group Limited
London · New York · Sydney · Toronto
Astronaut House, Feltham, Middlesex, England
Copyright © The Hamlyn Publishing Group Limited 1977

ISBN 0 600 36575 1 (cased edition)
ISBN 0 600 36585 9 (paperback edition)

Filmset in England by Tradespools Limited, Frome, Somerset
Printed in England

Contents

Preface

I suppose I was about four years old when I saw my first owl. I can still remember it very clearly indeed, even though I have forgotten everything else about that particular occasion. It was broad daylight and there, flying down a hedgerow, was a startlingly white bird – a Barn Owl. Many years were to pass before I saw another one, and that too was in broad daylight, but at much closer range. This time the bird was flying fast and trying to escape the attentions of an irate Jay and a number of other birds which had presumably found it at a roost site.

Of the few owl species to be seen in Britain, the Barn Owl has become my particular favourite. I have spent many happy hours watching Barn Owls hunting in daylight, especially on winter afternoons in parts of south-west Scotland where they are particularly common, and I am lucky enough to see them regularly in the dusk, either floating like ghostly white apparitions through my car headlight beams, or sitting watchfully on a fence or gate-post as I go past. I have not found them particularly wary of man and, indeed, by sitting or standing still, I have watched them hunting at very close range on a number of occasions. I have had one almost hit me in the face, and have a friend who has actually had one land on his head! They are particularly beautiful owls, as you will soon see if you examine a dead one, and it is a great pity that dead Barn Owls are all too frequently seen along our roads today.

But the first owl I came to know well was the Little Owl, probably because of its largely diurnal habits and certainly because two used to roost in the crown of an old oak near my home, often not moving for hours on end, and I saw them virtually every day. In my early years as a birdwatcher, I spent a lot of time watching Little Owls hunting along hedgerows and field edges and listening to their wild yelling and rather quiet, tooting song. I remember my thrill at finding an occupied nest for the first time, and my terror when I accidentally cornered a Little Owl in a big Heligoland trap at a bird observatory and it came at me talons-first in a bold (and successful) bid to escape!

The Tawny Owl is easily the most numerous and widespread British Owl, but it was one I did not get to know well until much later on. For years it remained just a voice in the dark, or at best a bird I glimpsed sometimes in the dusk or when I flushed one from a roost. By the time I had learned where to look for roosting Long-eared Owls in their winter hiding places I had already become addicted to owls as a group. Because I was also interested in the diurnal birds of prey, I wanted to know a lot more about their elusive nocturnal counterparts. So there followed numerous adventures with owls: plotting the territories of the local Tawnies; walking the great pine forests of Speyside in the black of night listening for Long-eareds; watching Barn Owls hunting in the bright winter sunlight in Gallo-way; and so on. The first exciting encounter with the Short-eared Owl, flushed from long grass on a sea wall on a bitterly cold winter's morning in Essex, duly receded in my mind as I watched these fine birds hunting and displaying over their northern moorlands, and trekked for many kilometres looking for their nests and roosting places. By this time, too, I was pulling pellets to pieces and teaching myself how to identify owl prey remains.

Then there were the first owls 'in the hand'. These were usually dead ones, often traffic victims, but sometimes there were live ones, too, again traffic casualties but also including a Tawny Owl which, incredibly, had been trapped in a chimney for the best part of a week before it was rescued! It is only when you handle an owl that you fully appreciate the thickness and softness of its plumage, as well as its beautiful markings, and that you discover that the body inside this outer covering is not as big and as plump as you thought it was going to be. You also see for the first time just how large and strong the hooked bill can be and, if you are unlucky, how sharp are the talons on those powerful feet. Another very striking thing is the mobility of the facial discs on a live owl, and the size of the bird's eyes. It can be a little difficult looking at the ears of a live owl, but with a dead one they can be examined in detail, and nobody can fail to be impressed by their quite extraordinary size. All this gives you a real insight into the special adaptations which these remarkable birds have evolved.

Somewhere in the literature, I had also read of the remarkable way in which some owls, when handled or frightened, 'freeze' and seem to feign death. Indeed, some American owls have even been lifted from their perches by ornithologists studying them, and have been weighed and measured, and have then been put back again! I was particularly interested when a Barn Owl I was handling 'froze' and became just like a corpse, closing its facial discs right in at the same time. The Tawny Owl from the chimney was even more remarkable, although it is the only one I have handled which has played dead in this way. After assuming a rather stiff posture in my hands, it even rolled over on its side when it was placed on the floor only to spring up and fly strongly round the room once I had retreated far enough.

These personal reminiscences illustrate well enough how easy it is to become fascinated by owls. There is a certain mysteriousness about them that is attractive to the enquiring mind, and finding out how they lead their daily lives and use their specially evolved eyesight and hearing can keep any ornithologist busy for years. It is, therefore, a little surprising to find that so few birdwatchers have become owl specialists, especially when we consider how many devotees there are for some other groups of birds, such as birds of prey and seabirds. Most ornithologists like seeing owls, but there are certain difficulties in getting to know the birds really well and this probably deters a lot of would-be researchers. Not the least problematical is the fact that so many owls are most active in the dark when we are singularly ill-equipped to detect them and to see what they are doing. Equally, in those areas where there are the most observers, the variety of owls is relatively small. In Europe, there are only thirteen breeding species (or a fraction under 10 per cent of the world's owls) and unless you live in some parts of Scandinavia some of these might just as well be on the other side of the world! Even North America, with its enormously wide range of habitat types, only boasts eighteen species, and some of these are either uncommon or very restricted in distribution.

Notwithstanding the problems, a few dedicated owl-watchers have made lifelong studies of a few species of owls. Man's inventiveness has come to their aid too to help them see in the dark, as their quarries can do without difficulty! What these few workers have found out about a small but representative selection of owls is dwarfed into insignificance by what we do *not* know about the rest. At best, we know quite a lot about a few species, a little about many more, and virtually nothing about the large remainder. One of the richest fields for ornithological research lies in making fuller studies of any of three-quarters of the world's owls and it is to be hoped that the growing interest in this order of birds may produce many interesting new facts in the years ahead. Some spirit of adventure often forms a useful ingredient to any natural history study – the problems in finding owls and the interesting regions where many of them occur should fulfil the needs of even the most adventurous ornithologist!

The work of this small band of owl enthusiasts forms the backbone of the information contained in this book. Indeed, without their industry in the field and the many papers and other publications they have produced, accounts such as this could not be written. No one person can claim to have a close knowledge of more than a few owl species at once. This book does not set out to be the last word on owls – nobody will say that for a very long time – nor does it have any pretensions towards being a fully authoritative text-book on owls. Instead, it is intended as an introduction to the owls aimed as much at the general reader as the interested naturalist. Following a summary of the little we know about owl origins and evolution, it discusses the distribution of modern owls and describes their breeding habits and their relationships with their prey. The unique ways in which they are adapted to their way of life are also examined and, finally, so are some of the problems faced by owls today.

It is an unfortunate fact that some owls *do* face a number of problems. While they have long been 'popular' birds in one sense, they have been completely misunderstood, too, and have become distinctly unpopular in some quarters. While a few species are regarded as allies of man, many more are persecuted quite needlessly and classed as vermin because of the damage to man's interests (more often the interests of a few men) they are alleged to do. Elsewhere, their habitat is fast disappearing or is undergoing rapid changes – in either case spelling disaster, particularly for some interesting owls found only in a few areas or on isolated islands. There is a growing need for the better conservation of some owls, even if the majority is, for the time being, in no immediate danger.

Above all, perhaps, there is a great need for man to understand owls. They have shared this planet with him for a very long time but for the most part he still shows rather little concern for them, even when they can be shown to be at least neutral to his own interests, if not actually beneficial. We could use almost the same words, indeed, of many other kinds of wildlife. More studies of owls will contribute to a better appreciation of them as living creatures in their own right as well as helping in the long term to save them if they become endangered.

The American naturalist/philosopher, Henry David Thoreau, once said, 'I rejoice that there are owls'. It was a good sentiment, and long may these fascinating birds of the night continue to intrigue us, to appeal to us, and to survive alongside us. Perhaps this book will go some way to furthering a general interest in owls and why there is some point in bothering about them; if it does, then it will achieve its objective.

Origins and evolution

Curiosity is a characteristic shared by all naturalists, whatever their age or status. Most, if not all, would admit to sharing a common curiosity about the origins of life on our planet – when and how it all began and, if they support the comparatively modern scientific notions of evolution and natural selection, how, when, and why all the wonderfully diverse forms of life we know today came about. Satisfying this particular aspect of our curiosity is a difficult and frustrating business, relying rather more on theory and speculation than on solid facts. It is as if we were trying to piece together an enormous jigsaw, knowing roughly what the final picture might look like but possessing so few pieces that discovering how they might relate to one another must remain an unsolved mystery.

Our knowledge of the origins and the subsequent evolution of birds is at best fragmentary. Fossil remains provide a few useful pieces for our jigsaw and we can make some more deductions from comparative studies of living birds, but huge gaps remain. Unfortunately, the study of bird evolution has never seemed quite as popular as that of mammals and reptiles, and even the study of the fossil remains we possess has been a neglected science. Furthermore, bird remains are rare and often poorly preserved. Birds have flimsy, lightweight bones which soon break down or are damaged so that they make poor fossils. They are best preserved in silty deposits associated with wetland habitats so that the best preserved examples are often those of birds which led aquatic lives or were at least partly associated with water. As if this were not enough, bird bones are notoriously difficult to identify – hard enough when they come from living forms and even more so when they occur as fossils. When our chances of making any meaningful comments on the history of birds are so slim, the possibility of doing so with a single group like the owls is even more difficult. We can at least summarize the available evidence, however, and make a few basic deductions.

Great Horned Owl – some of the earliest known fossil owls may have been closely related to this species.

Firstly, it is as well to digress briefly and explain the terms used in classifying owls. The system of naming and classifying living things which is now in international use is based on that devised by the eighteenth century Swedish naturalist Linné (or Linnaeus, as he is usually called). In this system each species has a unique 'scientific name', in Latinized form, which distinguishes it from all other species. The complex rules governing this system of nomenclature need not be discussed here – the essential point is that an internationally recognized set of scientific names exists which precludes the confusion which often arises from using vernacular names.

All birds are placed in the **class** Aves, which at once separates them from all other forms of life. The class is divided into various **orders** in which related **families** of birds are placed together. All the owls are placed together in the order Strigiformes which contains two families, the Tytonidae (barn and bay owls) and the Strigidae (all other owls). Families are further divided into **subfamilies** and indeed this happens with the owls, as shown in the list of owls of the world at the end of the book. The next important division within the family is the **genus** (*plural* genera) which brings together closely related forms and consists of one or more **species**. It is at species level that the unique scientific name applies and, as can be seen from the list, this consists of two words, the first, a noun, being the generic name and the second an adjective qualifying it. The two together is the complete species name. A further subdivision that you will meet later in this book involves placing another adjective against the species name to denote a **subspecies**, that is, a geographically separated form of a species.

To return to our theme, it is generally believed that birds evolved from certain small dinosaurs, although whether these were ground dwellers or tree-living forms is a matter of debate. Evidence pointing towards a reptilian ancestry is provided by the famous fossils of *Archaeopteryx lithographica*, the earliest known bird, whose remains were found in Upper Jurassic limestone and are thought to be about 160 million years old. This curious creature shows a number of distinctly reptilian features, but it also possessed features just like those of a modern bird and was clearly capable of at least limited flight. Unfortunately, there is then a considerable gap in the fossil record until the Cretaceous period of seventy to 100 million years ago when true bird forms appeared. So far, no fossil owl is definitely known from this period, but it seems possible that the earliest representatives of the order appeared during its latter stages.

Geologists date a whole new era, the Tertiary, from the end of the Cretaceous period, bringing us through five periods, the Palaeocene (seventy to sixty million years ago), the Eocene (sixty to forty million years ago), the Oligocene (forty to twenty-five million years ago), the Miocene (twenty-five to ten million years ago), and the

Pliocene (ten to three million years ago). It is during this era that more and more bird forms appeared and the class became increasingly diversified, and here too that we begin to trace the forerunners of modern owls and eventually to encounter representatives of genera we know today. Obviously, birds were not evolving in isolation during all these millions of years. Their increasing success and diversification must be seen against a background of much larger developments occurring during the Tertiary.

The Tertiary was an era of considerable geological and climatic change. From the point of view of bird evolution, it is important because it also saw a tremendous advance in the evolution of the angiosperms, or flowering plants, which have remained dominant over much of the Earth's land surface ever since. The last of the great dinosaurs had disappeared before the Tertiary began and the spread of many new forms of mammals began in earnest – culminating in the arrival of man during the Pliocene period. With the development and spread of forests and grasslands, many smaller mammals evolved to fill the niches which became available in these new habitats. Close behind came the predators which were to use them as a source of food. These included two important orders of birds: the Falconiformes, the birds of prey; and the Strigiformes – also birds of prey but of a somewhat different kind. Already the two orders were beginning to fulfil different roles, with the Falconiformes scavenging and hunting by day and the owls specializing in hunting by night.

Fossil remains which may yet prove to be

The Short-eared Owl is a living representative of a genus of owls which has existed for at least twenty-five million years.

those of owls are known from the first ten million years of the Eocene, but the oldest definitely identified remnants date from the remainder of this period and the ensuing Oligocene. The most ancient fossils identified so far have all been found in North America and represent five species which have been grouped into an extinct family of primitive owls known as the Protostrigidae. Seven more species of relatively more recent origin have been named from fossils found in France and are the earliest known representatives of the modern family Strigidae. All seven are extinct, but two seem to have resembled some owls we know today and have been assigned, provisionally, to the extant genera, *Bubo*, the eagle owls, and *Asio*, the eared owls.

During the Miocene period, the first members of the other modern owl family, the Tytonidae, made their appearance, with five species described from fossils found in France. Four more from the Strigidae have also been named, three from Europe and one from the United States, all of them extinct but all representing modern genera – *Bubo*, *Otus*, and *Strix*. The last period of the Tertiary, the Pliocene, has yielded

fossil remains of another extinct representative of the Tytonidae, this time from North America, and four more, also extinct, from the Strigidae, from both Europe and the United States. One of these is the earliest known example of yet another modern genus, *Speotyto*.

It was during the next period, the Pleistocene, which ended about 10000 years ago, that birds appear to have passed through an evolutionary acme with the development of more and more diverse species. Indeed, it is believed that they may have reached a peak about 500000 years ago when the number of species may have exceeded today's total by about one-third. Owl fossils from this period are relatively plentiful when compared with earlier times, so much so that forty-four species have been identified from all over the world – thirty of which are still in existence today. After the Pleistocene we enter the Holocene or Recent period from which many more owl species have been identified from finds made in prehistoric sites all over the world.

One feature which all fossil owl remains have in common is that they represent true owls: so far no owl-like fossils have been discovered which could give us any hints as to what other birds might share a common ancestor with the Strigiformes. This is one part of the jigsaw where all the pieces are missing at the moment so that the best we can do is to look at other orders known to us and try to discover whether any of them provides any clues to owl evolution and the relationships between owls and other birds.

The most obvious relatives of the owls might at first sight seem to be the diurnal birds of prey of the order Falconiformes. There are, after all, some striking similarities between the two groups. For instance, both are made up of specialist predatory birds with mostly powerful talons for killing live prey and strong, hooked beaks. Some other anatomical features are basically similar, but there are even more differences between the two orders and current thinking is that they may not be closely related at all but have simply evolved along roughly parallel courses. In doing so they have certainly achieved a remarkable interlocking function as the ultimate bird predators, the one group operating largely by day and the other largely by night, with only a small area of overlap. Almost every degree of specialization in sharing available prey species seems to have been achieved – with the diurnal birds of prey covering rather more of the spectrum than the owls.

It is interesting that the two groups within these orders which seem to be most closely related are both rather atypical of the orders as a whole – the true falcons on the one side and the barn and bay owls on the other. Certain similarities between them have kept systematists wondering for many years and, curiously enough, a new method of investigating interrelationships between birds has thrown up a clue which suggests that some kinship between these birds may exist after all.

This is the study of the proteins present in the whites of birds' eggs. While studies of owls' eggs show they are a closely-knit group of birds, they also indicate some similarities between true falcons and the barn and bay owls. They also show even more distinct possibilities of a link-up between owls and another order of nocturnal birds, the Caprimulgiformes, which includes the insectivorous nightjars, potoos, oilbirds, and their allies.

From what we know so far, it does seem likely that the Caprimulgiformes are the owls' nearest living relatives and that they may have evolved from a common ancestor. It remains possible that there is a relationship with the diurnal birds of prey after all. But until we find a lot more missing pieces for our jigsaw, our assumptions or conclusions regarding owl evolution and their place on the family tree of the class Aves must remain speculative.

The Snowy Owl seems to be a relatively modern species, the earliest fossils found so far dating from the Pleistocene period (three million to 10000 years ago).

Owls great and small

However they evolved and whatever their relationships with other birds, there is no doubt that owls are a successful group. With the exception of Antarctica and some islands, they have a more or less worldwide distribution in which they live in a wide variety of habitats. While many owls are associated to some degree with forests and woodland, or at least with trees, there are others which are just as much at home in open country, including even deserts and arctic tundras. They range in size from the sparrow-sized Elf Owl of the American West to the huge, powerful Eagle Owl of Eurasia and take a correspondingly wide variety of prey, from insects to surprisingly large mammals and birds. Perhaps two-thirds of them are essentially nocturnal, but others hunt just as well by day and many can do so at any time.

The adaptations which make owls such effective predators and which make them the nocturnal counterparts of the equally skilled day-hunting birds of prey are discussed more fully in the next chapter, but for the moment we can summarize the main features which go to make up an owl. Generally speaking, they appear as compactly built, robust birds with powerful legs and strong, hooked talons. They are relatively big headed with large, forward-facing eyes set in rounded facial discs. Owls appear neckless and their rounded outlines are produced by dense, soft feathering which effectively conceals the more traditionally shaped bird within. Anyone handling an owl for the first time will at once be struck by the slightness of the bird underneath this thick covering. Other very important features – the large and incredibly well-developed ears – are not at all obvious.

In any order of birds, there is always some dispute as to which members should be classified in the same genera, which should be regarded as full species, and which are best regarded as races or subspecies, and so on. This is as true of owls as of any other birds, but the classification and nomenclature used here follows that used in *Owls of the World*, the most recent standard work, edited by John Burton, whose list closely follows that proposed by J L Peters in Volume 4 of his *Birds of the World*, published in 1940, with some amendments arising from recent taxonomic work on certain species and genera. As we have mentioned already, the owls are divided into two families which between them include more than 130 species grouped in twenty-four different genera.

The family Tytonidae includes eight barn owls and two species of bay owls. All these birds differ from the owls of the main family, the Strigidae, in a number of minor ways and for this reason are usually considered distinct enough to merit their own family. The heart-shaped face of the barn owls – which is also present, though less complete, in the bay owls – is the most obvious feature not shared by other owls. Others are less easily observed, like the equal lengths of the second and third toes (the second is shorter in other owls) and the comb-like edge to the claw of the middle toe (absent in other owls). Internally, the breastbone and wishbone, clearly separated in other owls, are joined in the Tytonidae. There are other minor differences in plumage and bone structure.

There can be no doubt that the Common Barn Owl is the best-known member of the family, if not the best-known owl of all. It is one of a very small number of birds which has an almost worldwide distribution, being found in the Americas, over most of Europe south of Scandinavia, in North Africa and much of Africa south of the Sahara, in the Arabian peninsula and then, after a gap in its range, from India south-eastwards through south-east Asia to Australia. As many as thirty-four different geographical races of this one species are recognized, many of them confined to islands or island groups. All are basically similar in plumage – golden-buff above (darker or browner in some races) and white or pale below (pure white in some races, shading through various buffs, yellows, and oranges to rufous or even brown in others).

This is the ghostly 'white owl' so often seen in our car headlights as it floats silently across a country lane or hovers intently above a roadside verge. It is chiefly a bird of open countryside, but it is often strongly associated with human habitations through its habit of nesting in farm buildings, church towers, ruins, and the like. Of all the owls, this one, with its totally silent flight, its eerie appearance, its associations with ruins and churchyards, and its unearthly shrieks, is the bird most associated with superstition and folklore, even among civilized peoples. Tales about Barn Owls are legion, but not all are of the ghostly variety. The snores and hisses which are part of its large vocal repertoire led, in one instance known to the author, to a request from a country vicar that the owls be removed from his church as they were interrupting his services and (more likely, one suspects) his sermons!

The Common Grass Owl is a bird of open grassland occurring in Asia, Africa, and Australasia.

Little is known about the Sooty Owl; it is a bird of the dense forests of Australia and New Guinea.

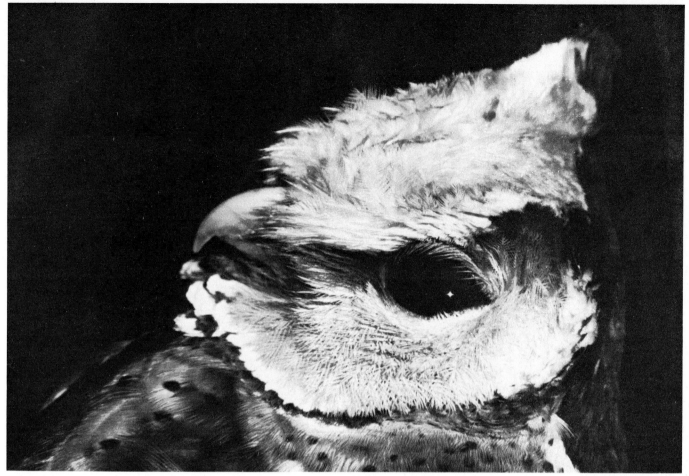

Of the other seven barn owl species, five are found in Australasia, one in that continent and also south-east Asia, India, and Africa, and the other on Madagascar.

The Common Grass Owl has the widest distribution and is, as its name implies, a bird of open grasslands. It resembles a Barn Owl in general appearance but is browner above and has even longer, almost naked legs which are presumably an adaptation to its largely terrestrial way of life. Like the Common Barn Owl, it is primarily a predator of small mammals. Some authorities consider the African form to be a different species to the forms elsewhere, calling the latter *Tyto longimembris* and recognizing a number of different races. The Madagascar Grass Owl is a very similar, though smaller and browner bird occurring only on that island.

Three more species have a very restricted distribution: the Celebes Barn Owl is a large bird of rainforest country on that island; while the northern part of Celebes is the home of the smaller Minahassa Barn Owl; finally, there is another rather small species found on one island only, the New Britain Island Barn Owl.

Australia, Tasmania, and part of New Guinea are the home of the Masked or Chestnut-faced Owl, a particularly large barn owl of forested country and open woodland with more open land nearby. The little-known and apparently rather rare Sooty Owl occurs in the eastern half of Australia and on New Guinea where it frequents dense forests. With its very dark plumage, it is a

distinctive bird when seen and it has relatively larger eyes than the other owls in its genus.

Any book on owls is bound to have one recurring statement – that a given species is little known or has not been studied in any detail by ornithologists. This is certainly true of the two bay owls which complete the family Tytonidae. The Common Bay Owl is found from northern India through south-east Asia to Indonesia and is apparently a forest species of strictly nocturnal habits. Very little is known of its life history. Until 1951 this was the only bay owl known, but then a specimen of what appears to be a distinct species, named the African Bay Owl, was collected in the eastern Congo: so far this is the only known example of this owl, which seems to be a bird of montane forests but is otherwise totally unknown. Like the eastern species, it has a compressed bill and, unlike the barn owls of open country, is a rather short-winged, woodland hunter.

The largest genus of the family Strigidae is *Otus*, the screech and scops owls, the former named from the call of one of the American species and the curious word 'scops' deriving from an Ancient Greek word for owls generally. Broadly speaking, screech owls are New World birds and scops owls belong to the Old World. Another broad distinction may be drawn from their voices, scops owls calling with a series of rather monotonous, short, single notes and screech owls making longer trills. All are rather less specialized than most other owls and on the

The curious-looking Common Bay Owl is another little-known forest owl, found from northern India and Sri Lanka through south-east Asia to Java and Borneo.

Although it is one of the best-known owls, the Eurasian Eagle Owl is a rare bird in many parts of Europe.

19

The dark-breasted form of the Barn Owl.

The Eurasian Scops
Owl is a small and
well-camouflaged
species.

whole are mainly nocturnal. They range in size
from small to medium – the largest being about
the size of a pigeon – and many are insectivorous.
A large proportion of these owls occurs in the
tropics but there are a few temperate zone
species; the latter tend to be the best studied and
the life histories of most of the rest are, at best,
little known. They are also rather difficult to
identify, few of them showing any really distinctive plumage features, so that their calls
become very important for identification purposes in areas where more than one species might
be encountered.

As in other genera, many of the *Otus* owls
occur in two distinct 'colour phases' – grey birds
and rufous birds. The former use their camouflage to roost up against the trunks of trees
while the latter do so in thick foliage. In North

The genus *Otus* contains many small owls with a mainly tropical distribution. One of the most handsome is the White-faced Scops Owl of the African savannahs.

America, grey-phase screech owls are associated more with conifers and habitats like mesquite scrub, while rufous birds prefer broadleaved trees and woodland.

Another difficulty with these owls is their classification. Authorities have different opinions on full species and subspecies within the genus, or on where to draw the lines between obviously closely related owls occurring close together in some regions. The appendix lists thirty-four species, following the recommendations of the Dutch ornithologist, G P Hekstra, who made a special study of the *Otus* owls, but no doubt their classification will remain a matter of debate until more research has been done on many of them.

New World screech owls can be divided into two main groups – those inhabiting the forests of Central and South America and those of more open woodland found all the way from Alaska down to Argentina. The first group includes a dozen species, all relatively little studied, which between them occupy different forest zones, areas of different altitude, density, and humidity, sharing out the ecological niches in these forests and, where more than one species occur close together, not competing for the same food sup-

ply. The Vermiculated Screech Owl is one of the most widely distributed, occurring from Mexico to Bolivia and Venezuela and boasting fifteen geographical races. The other screech owls in this first group have much more restricted ranges, although the Tawny-bellied Screech Owl is found over a large area of tropical forest in the Amazon region and into Guyana and central Brazil. One of the most local species is the Puerto Rican Screech Owl – now also one of the most endangered by the progressive felling of its forest habitat.

The second screech owl group contains birds found in more open, drier woodland areas, even extending into desert habitats. They tend to be paler in appearance than the forest owls and, like many predatory birds living in relatively open areas, have rather shorter tails than their forest-dwelling cousins. The longer tails of the forest owls and hawks help to provide them with greater manoeuvrability as they fly through dense vegetation.

In North America there are two species, the Eastern and Western Screech Owls, which occur respectively to the east of the Rocky Mountains (in mixed woodland) and to the west of this range (in woodland, scrub, and cactus desert) as far south as Mexico. They meet on the Rio Grande where they hybridize; indeed, some authorities regard them as races of a single species. Both have been well studied. They are largely insectivorous but also take small mammals and birds, reptiles, and assorted invertebrates. Birds in mountain areas tend to move down to lower ground in winter, but they are not truly migratory – unusual in non-tropical, insect-eating birds and unlike the European Scops Owl in this respect. In fact, birds living in the extreme north of the species' range are able to survive spells of very severe weather by simply ceasing to be active and by living on the fat they have accumulated in the autumn.

The other species in this group are the Roborate Screech Owl, found only in parts of Peru; the Pacific Screech Owl, occurring in a narrow coastal strip of mangrove forest and scrub from Mexico down to Costa Rica; and the Choliba Screech Owl which is found over a wide area of South America.

Notwithstanding the generalization made earlier, three Old World species bearing the name 'scops' might be better regarded as screech owls in type. The handsome White-faced Scops Owl is a bird of the African savannah with a wide distribution south of the Sahara, while the other two are oriental. The Giant Scops Owl is a forest species from the Philippines, and the White-fronted Scops Owl, another forest bird, is found in the Malay peninsula. The White-fronted has an exceptionally long tail for an *Otus* owl. These two scops owls are the largest members of the genus.

The scops owls of the Old World seem to have

Over much of Asia, the Collared Scops Owl occurs in lightly timbered areas and also frequents town gardens.

23

The Great Horned
Owl is the big eagle
owl of the Americas.

evolved in a similar way to their cousins in the
Americas and once again we meet a complex
pattern of species and/or subspecies, often with
isolated populations and differing slightly in their
choices of habitat. As with the screech owls, the
undoubted fact that so many of them are largely
unknown renders their classification difficult.

Over a large part of Asia, from Pakistan
through south-east Asia to the Philippines, the
Collared Scops Owl is a bird of lightly timbered
areas, even occurring in town gardens. In denser
forest in Malaysia it is replaced by the Reddish
Scops Owl while the species found at greater
altitudes is the Spotted Scops Owl. These two
species seem to be losing ground to the Collared
Scops Owl as the primary forest they inhabit is
progressively felled and this owl moves into the
newly colonizing timber and scrub. Various
isolated island species occur, the best known in
Asia being the Celebes Scops Owl; its counterpart on the western side of the Indian Ocean is
the Madagascan Scops Owl, which has races

(or possibly full species closely related to it) on
other islands.

The Oriental Scops Owl occurs in woodland
along rivers from the Holy Land across to
Turkestan, with another more eastern population found from India through to eastern
Siberia, Japan, and the Philippines – this population living in savannah, parkland, and dry
woodland. The more northern birds are fully
migratory, as is the case with the closely related
(and possibly conspecific) European Scops Owl,
which is found right across southern Europe and
into western Asia. This small owl, often heard
but seldom seen, inhabits open woodland, parks,
gardens, and even towns. Its monotonous song
is one of the most characteristic sounds of warm
Mediterranean evenings. It occurs again south
of the Sahara in African woodlands and savannah,
and some authorities treat this population as a
separate species. In North and Central America,
the little Flammulated Owl is the counterpart
of the Oriental and European Scops Owls. Other

A milky Eagle Owl with a hare. This large owl kills many good-sized mammals.

species with isolated populations occur in Africa, including the rare and only recently discovered Sokoke Scops Owl, and in the Orient, where the Spotted Scops Owl is perhaps the best known.

Two owls from another genus, *Lophostrix*, may be quite closely related to the *Otus* owls, and perhaps also to the South American spectacled owls of the genus *Pulsatrix*. These are the handsome Maned Owl, from the tropical forests of west Africa, and the equally striking Crested Owl, another forest owl found from southern Mexico down into central Brazil. Both of these medium-sized owls are probably mainly insectivorous but, once again, very little is known about them.

It is a considerable jump from the small owls of the preceding genera to the twelve species of eagle owls of the genus *Bubo*. Eagle owls are large and very powerful predators which, between them, occupy a very wide range of habitats and are found throughout the world, except on the arctic tundra where they are replaced by the equally large and impressive Snowy Owl, and in Australasia and the Pacific islands where their counterparts are some of the larger hawk owls. For the most part, these big, nocturnal owls take large prey – medium-sized birds of all sorts and mammals up to the size of hares, young deer, and even half-grown foxes.

The Eurasian Eagle Owl occurs over an enormous area, from northern Europe and the Iberian peninsula across most of Asia (including

25

The Eurasian Eagle
Owl is the largest
and most powerful
owl of all, able to
kill rabbits and much
larger prey, too.

India) to the Pacific coast, and in North Africa. In Europe, it is a bird of rocky terrain with forest cover or at least some timber, but elsewhere it may be a bird of tropical rainforest or even deserts. There is much variation in size and colour. The more northerly populations include the largest specimens, up to 710 millimetres (28 inches) in total length, the size gradually decreasing southwards over the species' range. The drier the habitat, the paler the plumage. There is an enormous difference between a large, richly coloured forest owl from northern Europe and a rather small, sandy coloured bird from the African deserts and, indeed, some authorities regard the race found in North Africa and the Middle East (the so-called Pharaoh Eagle Owl) and also that occurring in India as separate species. The largest owls in the world are female Eurasian Eagle Owls from the more northerly populations.

Almost as large, and occupying an even wider range of habitats, from swampland and rainforest in tropical regions to boreal forests in Canada and Alaska, the Great Horned Owl is the counterpart of the Eurasian species in the

Americas. It is the only New World *Bubo* and is found from subarctic Canada almost all the way to the extreme tip of South America. It takes its name from its conspicuous 'ear-tufts', a feature common to all the owls of this genus.

Six more eagle owls occur in Africa south of the Sahara, occupying various habitats but not being as adaptable in this respect as the previous two species. The Cape Eagle Owl is a bird of high mountain areas of mixed forest and open terrain, with isolated populations in upland areas down the eastern side of the continent, but also coming down to sea-level at the Cape. At lower altitudes over the main part of its range, its place is taken by the Spotted and Milky Eagle Owls, both widespread species, the former preferring rocky areas with light woodland and savannahs and the latter much denser riverain forest. The three other species are all birds of equatorial forest and have in common rarity and the fact that very little is known about them. One of these, the Akun Eagle Owl, is possibly insectivorous, while another, Fraser's Eagle Owl, seems to take a wide range of medium-sized prey. As it is a very large, powerful species, presum-

ably Shelley's Eagle Owl can tackle larger prey, perhaps up to the size of small forest antelopes.

The Dusky Eagle Owl is found in India and south-east Asia in riverain forest and other wooded or lightly timbered areas and more or less corresponds in choice of habitat with the African Milky Eagle Owl. Three more species occur in areas of forest with high rainfall – the Forest Eagle Owl (India, the Himalayas, Indochina), the Malaysian Eagle Owl, and the Philippine Eagle Owl, where, rather than occupying different ecological niches in the same region, they live in geographically separate areas.

Although they approach the great *Bubo* owls in size and strength, the owls of the two genera *Ketupa* and *Scotopelia* are very different in life style: these are the fish owls of Asia and Africa respectively, specialist feeders which are the nocturnal equivalents of the Osprey and the fish eagles.

The Asian species are found in all sorts of habitats close to water, from cold northern forests to equatorial jungle, where they feed on large fish and other aquatic creatures. Unlike most owls, their feet are naked of feathers and specially adapted for gripping their slippery prey, and they have less obvious facial discs than other species, presumably because hearing is not

Pel's Fishing Owl is the nocturnal equivalent of the Osprey and the fish eagles.

27

One of the few real
specialists among
owls – the Brown
Fish Owl from Asia.

Above
A sleepy Milky
Eagle Owl photo-
graphed in the
Kalahari National
Park.

Left
South-east Asia is
the home of the small
and very distinctive
Malaysian Eagle
Owl.

The unmistakable
Spectacled Owl –
one of the many owls
whose life history
is so far little known.

very important to them in capturing their prey. Similarly, they have little need for the silent flight so characteristic of other owls and therefore lack the very soft, sound-deadening plumage.

There is some overlap in the distribution of the Brown Fish Owl (parts of the Middle East, eastwards to India and Indochina), the Malaysian Fish Owl, and the Tawny Fish Owl (Himalayas, southern China and parts of Indochina), but for the most part they are well separated geographically. Where they coincide, the Brown and Malaysian species seem to occupy different habitats although both are found in all sorts of areas where there is water. Being a bird of upland forest streams and rivers, however, the Tawny Fish Owl hardly competes with either. Blakiston's Fish Owl is well separated, occurring in eastern Siberia and north-east China. It also differs from the others in having fully feathered legs, and is apparently more prone to seek its prey by wading in shallow water. The others do this too, but more often hunt from a vantage point overlooking the water, swooping down to take their prey in their talons from the surface.

Not a great deal is known about these curious Asian owls, and even less is known about their three African cousins of the genus *Scotopelia*.

These, too, are large, powerful owls, similarly equipped for dealing with fish, but they differ from the *Ketupa* owls in lacking ear-tufts and instead having loosely feathered, rather shaggy looking heads. Pel's Fishing Owl is a very large, spectacular-looking owl, rich, rufous-orange in colour, found over most of Africa south of the Sahara, while the Vermiculated Fishing Owl occurs only in strips of riverain forest (but not in the main, continuous forest) of the Congo. It is

The Malaysian Fish Owl is another expert 'fisherman' but, like all its relatives, it also preys on a variety of other aquatic animals.

31

The Starling-sized
Eurasian Pygmy Owl.

The Ferruginous
Pygmy Owl of
tropical America.

apparently a rare species, but not so rare or restricted in distribution as the Rufous Fishing Owl which is so far known only from a few specimens found in the rainforest from Sierra Leone to Ghana.

The spectacled owls of the genus *Pulsatrix* are much more 'typical' owls. All three are medium-large forest birds, mainly nocturnal, and, like so many owls, opportunist hunters feeding on a wide range of prey including birds, mammals, insects, and amphibians. They are relatively colourful owls and have dark faces outlined by paler 'spectacles'. Not much is known about any of them, but the large Spectacled Owl, found from southern Mexico down to Argentina, occurs in tropical rainforests and sometimes quite commonly in cultivated areas nearby. No doubt the other two, the White-chinned Owl (southern Brazil) and the Rusty-barred Owl (Ecuador and Peru) are similar in habits, but both seem to be rather rare and have not been studied at all.

In arctic regions, on the tundra beyond the limit of tree growth, the ecological niche filled by the eagle owls at lower latitudes is taken up by the handsome Snowy Owl, a large and powerful species which feeds principally on lemmings and Arctic Hares but also takes various other small mammals and a variety of birds up to the size of Eider Ducks. It has a circumpolar distribution and in some winters (as explained in a later chapter) may occur far to the south of its normal range. Since 1967 a single pair has nested in Shetland. The Snowy Owl is often a diurnal hunter because it lives in regions where daylight is prolonged or continuous in summer, though in other circumstances it tends to favour twilight for its feeding expeditions.

Another northern owl with a circumpolar distribution, but this time in semiwooded and scrubby areas of the arctic and subarctic regions, is the Hawk Owl. This, too, is a daytime hunter but even more so than the Snowy Owl. It looks like an owl in general appearance, but gets its name from its rather hawk-like physique (it is medium sized with rather pointed wings and a long, tapering tail) and behaviour. Hawk Owls fly swiftly, sometimes hovering, and usually hunt their small mammal prey with a quick swoop from a high vantage point. Like Snowy Owls, their movements are very much governed by the seasonal abundance of their prey and they, too, may occur well beyond their usual range in some years.

At the opposite end of the scale from the big eagle owls we find many very small species, among them the twelve pygmy owls of the genus *Glaucidium*. Many of them are at least partly diurnal and for all their small size they are highly efficient hunters of small mammals, birds, and insects, the latter two being caught on the wing in some cases. They sometimes even kill animals larger than themselves.

The most widespread and probably the best known is the Eurasian Pygmy Owl, a more nocturnal species than most *Glaucidium* owls,

found in open areas of coniferous or mixed forest in a wide band from Scandinavia and western Europe across Russia to Mongolia and Manchuria. From western Canada down the western fringes of the United States to Guatemala, the Northern Pygmy Owl is the counterpart of the Eurasian species though it often occurs in much more open habitats. Another similar species is the Ferruginous Pygmy Owl, found from Arizona and Texas to Chile and southern Argentina, while a third New World member of the genus is the Least Pygmy Owl,

The tiny Elf Owl is a desert species from southern North America.

33

found from Mexico and Central America discontinuously down to Brazil. The other New World species, the Cuban Pygmy Owl, is restricted to Cuba and the Isle of Pines.

Four species, all 'owlets', represent the genus in Africa. The Barred Owlet is rather larger than most *Glaucidium* owls and the Chestnut-backed Owlet is bigger still – though, at 250 millimetres (10 inches), it is still a small owl. There are three more in Asia, of which the Collared Pygmy Owl is the most widespread and, being largely diurnal, the best known. The Cuckoo Owlet, a rather larger species, is worthy of mention because it is said to be particularly agile and hawk-like, even capable of taking such fast-flying birds as Quail on the wing.

The tiny Elf Owl, alone in its own genus *Micrathene*, shares with the Least Pygmy Owl the distinction of being the smallest owl of all. Both species are a mere 130 millimetres ($5\frac{1}{8}$

inches) or so in length, only sparrow sized but fully fledged birds of prey for all that. The Elf Owl is confined to the south-west of the United States and Mexico, and although it occurs in woodland, forest, grassland, and wet savannahs, it is perhaps best known for its association with the giant *Saguaro* cactus in which it nests in cavities and, especially, holes made by woodpeckers. It is largely nocturnal and feeds principally on insects.

Although they are not closely related to the Hawk Owl described earlier, the sixteen species of the genus *Ninox* (the second largest owl genus) are all hawk owls in type. None is particularly large, some are quite small, and they vary quite a lot in the degree to which they look hawk-like. They all have proportionately smaller heads than most other owls, however, with very poorly developed or only rudimentary facial discs and small, symmetrical ear openings. Because facial

Left
One of the most strikingly marked of all owls is the Spectacled Owl from South America.

Above
Riverside forests in the Congo basin are the home of the Vermiculated Fishing Owl, one of three little-known African species.

35

The Barred Owl is
the American
counterpart of the
Ural Owl of Europe
and northern Asia.

The Tawny Owl is a
familiar species
across much of
Europe and Asia.

The big Snowy Owl is an arctic species and is one of the main bird predators of the tundra zone.

discs are associated with hearing, this points towards sight as being the more important sense to these owls when hunting.

The genus is a rather complex one in terms of the interrelationships between its members but, in geographical terms, they are mostly separated from one another and there is very little actual overlapping between species. Only one, the Oriental Hawk Owl, has a really wide range, being found over a considerable area of mainland Asia including India and Malaysia. It feeds on a great variety of prey and, comparatively, is one of the better known *Ninox* owls.

Three more species which have also been studied in some detail all occur in the southern part of Australasia, where their ranges overlap to some extent but, because they differ in size and choice of habitat, they do not compete with one another for prey. The smallest is the widely distributed Boobook Owl, found in Australia, New Zealand, and New Guinea, which is mainly an insect eater but also takes a variety of small

The Saw-whet Owl is a small North American woodland species.

Far left
Like the Snowy Owl, the Hawk Owl of the northern forest zone often hunts in broad daylight.

Left
The Cuckoo Owlet is one of a dozen species of pygmy owls; it is an Asian bird and one of the largest of the group.

Left
The Barred Owlet occurs in savannah country and is one of four African species of pygmy owl.

Right
Found only in the lowland forests of New Guinea, the Sooty-backed Hawk Owl is one of a number of owls of the genus *Ninox* found in Asia and Australasia.

mammals and birds. Next in size comes the Barking (or Winking) Owl, a much less widespread bird of forests and savannah, a mammal feeder with facial discs that are so rudimentary that they are actually less obvious than those of some of the diurnal birds of prey, such as harriers, that rely on hearing while hunting. The awesome-sounding Powerful Owl or Great Hawk Owl is the largest of the three and is even less owl-like in appearance than the Barking Owl. It is also much less common, being found only in forested gullies in south-east Australia.

Further north in Australia and in New Guinea,

the somewhat smaller Rufous Owl fills the niche of the Powerful Owl in thick woodland and rainforest, while in the lowland forests of New Guinea and some of its associated islands the Boobook Owl (which itself occurs in some parts of New Guinea) is replaced by the Sooty-backed Hawk Owl. Hawk owls, which must have evolved from a common stock and have developed far enough to become full species, have populations confined to a number of islands in the region. Thus, there is the Solomon Islands Hawk Owl and other species named after the Admiralty Islands, New Ireland (this one also occurs on

The Spotted Little
Owl is found in a
wide variety of habi-
tats from parts of the
Middle East to
south-east Asia.

The Boobook or
Morepork Owl is
probably the best
known of the *Ninox*
hawk owls and is
found in Australia,
New Zealand, and
New Guinea.

42

The unique Burrowing Owl, a long-legged, ground-dwelling species from the Americas.

New Britain), New Britain, the Moluccas (where the Barking Owl also occurs), the Philippines, and the Andaman Islands (where the Oriental Hawk Owl is also found). Two small species occur on Celebes, the common and widespread Speckled Hawk Owl and the rather rare and largely unknown Ochre-bellied Hawk Owl of the virgin forest country.

Two more hawk owls are sufficiently different from and more specialized than the *Ninox* species to have been placed in their own genera – the Papuan Hawk Owl (*Uroglaux*) and the Laughing Owl (*Sceloglaux*). Very little is known about the Papuan bird but it is apparently a lowland forest hawk owl and has a very long tail. It is known to feed on insects and small mammals. The Laughing Owl, a comparatively large hawk owl with a catholic taste in prey, was probably once a widely distributed bird over much of New Zealand where it inhabited rocky areas, either in the open or alongside woodland and forest. It is one of a number of birds found only in New Zealand which has suffered drastically from the invasions of man and the animals he has brought with him. Several decades have passed since the Laughing Owl was last seen and it is probably now extinct.

Because it is often active and visible long before dark, and is often seen at the roadside, the rather plump, flat-crowned Little Owl is perhaps the most familiar owl to people living in many areas of western Europe. It is one of three members of the genus *Athene*, a bird found in a wide variety of lightly timbered and open habitats, including dry rocky areas, ranging from England in the west (where it was introduced in the late 1800s), across Europe south of the Baltic, and through North Africa, across to Russia and western Asia, and as far as Mongolia and China

in the east. Unlike many owls, it is quite at home on the ground where it moves quickly and often runs in pursuit of small prey. From southern Iran into India and south-eastwards into Indochina, it is replaced by the Spotted Little Owl, a very similar species in many respects. The Forest Little Owl, from the dense forests and jungles of north-eastern and central India, is rather similar to its two cousins but it is generally rather darker and somewhat shorter in the wing – both adaptations to its life in forests rather than open country.

The unique Burrowing Owl (genus *Speotyto*) is very like the little owls in appearance and is closely related to them. It is a long-legged, basically terrestrial owl, found in open, treeless prairie country from western North America right down to the southern extremities of South America, with isolated populations in the Caribbean and in Florida. The burrows of prairie-dwelling mammals make instant homes for this owl, but it is able to excavate its own if the need arises. Insects, especially large beetles, and small rodents are the main prey, augmented by small birds and frogs from time to time.

Woodland and forest are the common link between the next two genera to be considered, *Ciccaba* and *Strix*. These birds, along with members of some other genera, such as *Pulsatrix*, are often collectively called 'wood owls'.

The five *Ciccaba* owls are birds of the tropical forests of Africa and the Americas. They have no ear-tufts or 'horns' on their well-rounded heads and, being mainly nocturnal, they show the well-developed facial discs characteristic of truly night-hunting owls. Not a great deal is known about any of them.

From Mexico down to north-eastern Argentina, the Mottled Owl is a bird of heavily

43

timbered areas, in mountain country and at lower altitudes, varying a great deal in size and colour from place to place. It is apparently an 'all-rounder' like so many owls, preying on small mammals, birds, reptiles, and insects. Three more species occurring in the New World are even less known than the Mottled Owl. The Black and White Owl is largely insectivorous and favours the edges of forests right through its range of southern Mexico to western Ecuador. The Black-banded Owl is found in the forests of the Amazon but shows interesting signs of being able to adapt to changing habitats by its regular appearance in banana and coffee plantations. The Rufous-banded Owl occurs in the more temperate, humid forests of the Andes from Venezuela into Ecuador.

The only Old World member of this group is the African Wood Owl which lives in forests and woodlands over a wide area south of the Sahara, at various altitudes and levels of humidity. It, too, takes a wide variety of prey animals.

In temperate forests and woodlands, the *Ciccaba* owls are replaced by the eleven *Strix* species whose distribution extends to every continent except Australia. Some of these owls are among the best-known and most extensively studied members of the order. For the most part, they are thoroughly nocturnal, with their large, rounded heads carrying all the special apparatus for night work – large eyes giving exceptionally good night vision, and large ears and pronounced facial discs providing quite incredible hearing. As we shall see in the next chapter, some of these owls are known to be fully capable of locating and capturing their prey by hearing alone.

The largest member of the genus (and to many owl-oriented ornithologists the most magnificent of all owls) is the Great Grey Owl, a bird of the northern forests of America and Eurasia – the only *Strix* owl found in the Old and New Worlds. Its disproportionately large head and relatively small eyes give it an appearance unique among owls, and yet all is not as it seems with this remarkable bird. It approaches the great eagle owls in size but is a relative lightweight, much of its apparent bulk being made up of exceedingly thick plumage which provides insulation against the often intense cold in the regions where it lives. It is often a diurnal hunter and, again surprisingly for such a large species, preys largely on voles and other small mammals.

Another Eurasian species, largely northern in distribution but with isolated populations further south (for example, in parts of Yugoslavia and China), is the Ural Owl, a bird of old coniferous forests and mixed woodland but one which also occurs close to human habitation in some areas. It is much less specialized in its choice of prey than the Great Grey, as is its New World counterpart the Barred Owl, which is found mainly in central and eastern North America but ranges south into Central America. In the north, it is found in similar kinds of habitat to the Ural Owl, but further south it is often associated with water in the denser forests where it then also preys upon crayfish, frogs, and fish. The other North American owl in this genus is the Spotted Owl, a rather scarce bird with a western pattern of distribution in dense forest and wooded gorges from British Columbia down to central Mexico. Two more species, both little known, are South American, the Brazilian Owl and the Rufous-legged Owl, the latter occurring from Argentina to Tierra del Fuego.

One of the most familiar of all the Old World species is the Tawny Owl which is essentially a bird of broadleaved woodland, parks, and towns. It has a very wide range, being found over most of Europe, in north-west Africa, the Middle East, and the Himalayas through to the mountains of Burma and China; in these more eastern regions it is a bird of coniferous forests. Though mainly a predator of small mammals, birds, frogs, and worms, it is a highly adaptable bird, even taking fish on occasion. The author has even seen one feeding on a dead rabbit (killed by traffic) in the middle of a road in broad daylight! Hume's Tawny Owl is a closely related species which perhaps replaces the Tawny Owl in some of the more arid and rocky areas of the Middle East, but it is one of the least-known birds of any kind in the world. It is doubtful whether any naturalist has seen one alive in the wild in the Middle East where it is known from a handful of specimens collected in different localities, and nothing at all is known about its distribution in Baluchistan where it was originally discovered a century ago. Perhaps the rapidly growing interest in the ornithology of the Middle East will shed some light on this mysterious bird before too long.

The Brown Wood Owl is one of three Asian species, found from India down into Indochina and Malaysia, in south China and in Taiwan and Hainan. Temperate deciduous forest is its preferred habitat over much of its range, but it also occurs in evergreen forests and, in Borneo, in lowland primary forest. It is a versatile predator which takes a very considerable variety of prey, even including up to the size of pheasants and jungle fowl. The Mottled Wood Owl is an Indian species found mainly in open, semi-cultivated areas, while the Spotted Wood Owl is a lowland bird in Malaysia.

The little-known Striped Owl (genus *Rhinoptynx*) is found in lowland forest from Mexico down to Bolivia and Brazil and its precise status in owl systematics is interesting: it resembles the *Asio* owls mentioned below, but also seems to form a link between the two families, the Tytonidae and the Strigidae. It is apparently mainly a mammal eater.

The five *Asio* owls may be separated into two categories – the 'long-eared' and 'short-eared' groups, these names referring to the ear-tufts which are a feature of many owl species. As discussed later, these erectile tufts of feathers which look to many of us just like ears are not connected with hearing at all.

The Long-eared Owl has a wide distribution across North America, and from Europe across

The Barred Owl is a relatively large wood owl from North and Central America.

45

Asia to Japan. It also occurs in parts of Africa, where it is usually given subspecific status but is treated as a different species by some authorities. Although it is often thought of as a bird of coniferous woodland, in many parts of its range it also occurs in broadleaved woodland, timber in cultivated areas, extensive thickets, and so on. Indeed, it is actually a fairly adaptable bird, nesting in heather in the open in Shetland where trees are very few and far between. Small mammals are the main prey of this strictly nocturnal bird, but in many areas small birds figure extensively in its diet. The Madagascar Long-eared Owl is a very closely related species found only on that island, while from Mexico to northern Argentina there is another close relative in forests and mountain woodlands, the large, dark Stygian Owl. That this too may be an adaptable bird is suggested by the fact that it also takes to ground nesting in treeless areas, as in Cuba.

The Short-eared Owl is essentially a diurnal species of open country, especially moorland, extensive grasslands and marshlands, with the long wings characteristic of many birds of prey which hunt in this kind of habitat. It is found in subarctic and temperate regions in North America and Eurasia, and again in the southern half of South America. In addition it has isolated populations on a number of islands such as the Galápagos and Hawaii. This owl feeds mainly on small mammals, as does its counterpart the African Marsh Owl, a bird of similar habitat in north-west Africa and in separate regions in the west, east, and south of the continent.

Two owls which are the sole representatives of their genera pose a number of unanswered questions regarding their relationships with other species. The Jamaican Owl (*Pseudoscops*), once thought to be closely linked with the scops and screech owls, may be more closely allied to the *Asio* owls described above. Some authorities think otherwise, however, and link it with still other genera. It is found only in Jamaica and is a highly nocturnal species, occurring in both woodland and open country. The Fearful Owl (*Nesasio*), found only on three islands in the Solomons (Australasia) is another enigmatic bird: in the lowland forests where it lives it apparently takes relatively large prey, for which it is equipped with exceptionally powerful talons and beak, so that it seems to fill the niche occupied elsewhere by the big eagle owls. Like so many owls, it requires study before its true ecological position can be evaluated.

Last, but by no means least, comes the genus *Aegolius* which contains four species of small owls. Two of these, the Unspotted Saw-whet Owl (southern Mexico to south-eastern Costa Rica) and the Buff-fronted Owl (north-western South America, southern Brazil, and northern

Open country, including wetlands, is the preferred habitat of the African Marsh Owl.

Tengmalm's or
Boreal Owl is a bird
of the northern
coniferous forests of
both the Old and
New Worlds.

Argentina) are largely unknown, but the other two have been looked at in some detail.

Tengmalm's Owl, which is called the Boreal Owl in North America, is yet another bird of coniferous forests in the northern regions of both the Old and the New Worlds. Except in the extreme north where daylight is continuous in summer, it is a highly nocturnal owl which feeds on small mammals and birds. The other species, the Saw-whet Owl (named from its 'saw-sharpening' call) is found only in the New World and is in effect the replacement species of the Boreal Owl in dense and often damp woodland, mainly to the south of that species' range in Alaska, Canada, and the United States. This, too, is a largely nocturnal species, again feeding on small birds and mammals.

Such, then, is the range of owls found throughout the world – a diverse and sometimes bewildering collection of owls of all sizes, preying on a very wide variety of animals in many quite different habitats. Not all are nocturnal, but most are at least partly so and many are singularly well equipped to live the most active parts of their lives in darkness. In the following chapters we shall look more closely at these special features which make owls what they are and then examine the way of life of some of the better-known species in greater detail. Finally, we shall examine their relationships with man – very often a close neighbour of owls, usually a somewhat mystified or indifferent one, sometimes benevolent towards them, and, rather too often in some regions, their most deadly enemy.

47

The anatomy of owls

It is easy enough to think of owls as friendly looking, even rather cuddly creatures. They sit upright, which perhaps makes them seem a little more familiar in human terms than most birds, and they often have rather plump forms, or at least rounded outlines. They have faces which can, without too much imagination, be seen as caricatures of our own with those round, staring eyes and beaks positioned just where noses ought to be. There is something reassuring, too, about their seemingly placid appearance, the way they sit almost without moving as we look at them, giving a slow, disdainful wink every now and then. To most people they are attractive birds and it is small wonder that they appear so often in cartoons or as soft children's toys. Even the most hardened, critical naturalist cannot fail to be moved.

In fact what we see is only coincidentally man-like, a product of our innate wish to see something of ourselves reflected in the wild creatures with which we share this planet: this is known as 'anthropomorphism'. We are really looking at a highly efficient predatory bird and all those features which catch our eye are actually the outward signs of its truly remarkable adaptation towards a life in the darkness. The big eyes set in their facial discs, and the ears which we cannot see at all, are parts of the highly specialized equipment the owl possesses to enable it to find and then kill its prey in light conditions which would leave us helpless. Even the remarkable immobility of the bird has its purpose.

As we have already seen, owls come in all sizes and exploit many varied habitats and food sources. In so doing, they take over the role of bird predators when the daylight has gone and most of the diurnal birds of prey have ceased to be active. The 'change-over' is not really as clear-cut as this because some owls are abroad early in the evenings or around dusk when some falcons or small hawks may still be busy catching insects or chasing small birds as they go to roost. Some small birds of prey also chase bats, but very few owls can cope with such fast-moving and elusive prey. Once true darkness sets in,

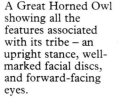

A Great Horned Owl showing all the features associated with its tribe – an upright stance, well-marked facial discs, and forward-facing eyes.

however, the owls have the field to themselves, with only their cousins the nightjars sharing the abundance of night-flying insects with them.

The very darkness in which owls are so much at home does nevertheless place some restrictions on them: they are not nearly as variable in design as the diurnal birds of prey, nor do they actually feed on such a wide range of prey in quite the same way. For example, many of the day-hunting birds of prey specialize in pursuing and capturing other birds in flight and only a few of the owls attempt this sort of thing, even then doing it in an opportunist way rather than regularly. Most birds eaten by owls are taken by stealth while they are roosting, so that the method of capture does not differ too much from that used to capture small mammals and insects. This is not to say that some owls are not quite good at catching birds when they can see them – the diurnal Snowy and Short-eared Owls, for instance, can be very adept at this sort of thing when the opportunity presents itself. Also, no owl specializes in carrion feeding in the way that vultures and some other birds of prey do, nor is there among the owls any 'general scavenger' corresponding to some of the kites and small vultures. Various mammals and a whole host of insects take over this role by night. The prey available to most owls conforms to a fairly basic pattern of movement and habit so that owls have evolved accordingly. There is really no need for some of the more extreme developments seen among the diurnal raptors which have to cope with a wider range of situations.

Most owls do not require the often strikingly coloured or patterned plumage seen in so many other birds because they are mostly active in darkness, or at least in indifferent light. Pattern and colour are functional in birds, not merely decorative, and present a number of visual signals to other birds and animals which work in a variety of ways, for courtship displays, threatening behaviour, individual recognition, and so on. It is difficult for us to comprehend that in many animals, birds included, a whole 'visual language' has developed, based on colour, pattern, and behaviour, in addition to vocalizations which are far removed from what we call speech. It is a common mistake to assume that animals are not particularly sophisticated in their communications simply because their vocal 'language' is so very restricted. In the darkness there are obviously limitations to how far owls can use a purely visual language to communicate with one another, and for this reason, many of them are rather soberly dressed although there are a few exceptions. Equally, there is little need for purely visual recognition between the sexes so that in almost every owl species the two are alike in appearance. General shapes, some movements, and especially voice are far more important. Owls are particularly vocal birds – much more so than the diurnal birds of prey – and we shall return to this aspect later.

It is perhaps appropriate at this point to come back to the ear-tufts which, as we have already said, are not connected with hearing at all but merely suggest external ears to us from their position on an owl's head. Those owls that have

Note the erect ear-tufts on this roosting Screech Owl; they are used as a form of visual communication and have no connection with hearing.

them in some form or another (and this means just under half the world's owl species) use them as a form of visual communication. They are very mobile and can be raised and lowered at will, so that just what one owl is doing with its ear-tufts can tell another owl a great deal about its 'mood' or intentions. How this works can be seen when a Long-eared Owl is found at a roost. When the owl is undisturbed, it sits in a relaxed position with the ear-tufts depressed and lying flat along the top of its head. It is nevertheless alert, listening all the while. As soon as it is disturbed, up come the ear-tufts, slowly and tentatively at first as the bird assesses the source of the disturbance and then reaching a near-vertical position when the owl identifies the intruder and watches and waits to see what will happen next. In other words, the movement of the ear-tufts is a response to possible danger (among other things) and no doubt also serves to tell other owls roosting nearby that something is wrong.

Colour and pattern in birds have another very important function which is quite the opposite of advertisement: this is camouflage, developed in so many wonderful ways that it merits a book on its own, and of the utmost importance to many birds as the chief means they have of escaping detection and capture by their enemies. Camouflage, or **cryptic coloration** as it is often called, is a feature of the plumage of most owls. It is of no particular relevance at night, of course, but it is most important to its owners in daylight when they are at their most vulnerable.

Some owls may be very active around dawn and dusk, but many of them spend the greater part of the daylight hours resting and sleeping. They like to do so in peace and quiet and they usually select roosting places which are well hidden, or rely on their well-developed cryptic patterns and colours to conceal them, or both. Even to the ornithologist who knows owls they can be very hard to find and even the tell-tale evidence of droppings and piles of pellets which accumulate at regular roost sites may only indicate that owls are in the area: they can be very hard to spot against a tree trunk or in dense foliage.

One of the basic principles of camouflage involves breaking up the outline so that the shape of the subject becomes indistinct, or even resembles something else, and the various patterns of barring, spotting, and streaking found in owls, plus some more obvious markings, achieve this very successfully. It is also vital to avoid contrasts, thus a largely white Barn Owl roosting in an oak would stand out in sharp contrast. As it happens, this particular owl prefers to roost inside holes in trees or rocks, or often inside buildings, and camouflage is not very important to it. Woodland owls tend to be generally brown or grey in basic colouring, being darkest when they occur in the very dense vegetation of tropical forests, and as a general rule birds found in coniferous woodland are rather greyer than those living in broadleaved trees.

Owls living in open habitats are typically paler in colour and are distinctly sandy coloured where they live in desert country. As we have seen, members of the same species can differ markedly in colour depending on the type of terrain in which they live. A Snowy Owl in a zoo (which is where most of us will have our only chance to see one) is a really strikingly coloured bird, but set it in its proper context among the rocks and snow patches of the arctic tundra and it becomes a wholly different proposition. Even the pure white male is by no means as obvious as might be supposed.

Contrast is also avoided by countershading which, in addition, reduces the three-dimensional appearance of a bird and renders it rather 'flatter' in form. In natural situations, most light falls on the upper surfaces of a bird's body and its underparts are, comparatively speaking, in shadow: the contrast this would present in a more or less uniformly coloured bird is often reduced by the underparts being decidedly lighter than the upperparts. This works well in most birds which are more or less 'horizontal' when standing or perching, but the principle has to be varied for owls which usually sit upright. Because as much light falls on their breasts as their backs, owls are countershaded rather differently, with the palest areas on their bodies being located from their bellies down towards their feet. It is interesting to note that in the Short-eared Owl, which characteristically adopts a markedly horizontal stance, the more normal form of countershading applies.

The most subtle camouflage in the world would be of little use if its owner was constantly moving or changing position: the very act of movement would soon reveal the animal. Therefore, the successful use of camouflage very often depends on immobility and in this respect owls are expert – the very stillness we remarked upon earlier is not a sign of a phlegmatic temperament but an aspect of owl behaviour which can be vital to its survival. Unless an owl is disturbed, it will sit motionless for long periods, and even when it does move it does so slowly and deliberately – there are no sudden movements as it looks around through half-closed eyes or keeps up its endless vigil of listening for new sounds which might spell danger. Any birdwatcher who has looked for roosting owls can tell his or her own stories about immobile birds escaping detection until some tiny movement gave them away – or until the bird actually flew off. The author once noticed a Tawny Owl in a thickly leaved tree because it blinked, and in a very dense hawthorn thicket only became aware of a Long-eared Owl very close to him because he suddenly saw its ear-tufts being erected where none had been visible before!

The Long-eared Owl provides a good illustration of all the points we have made concerning concealment. In coniferous woodland, it often roosts close to the main trunk of a tree, looking basically owl-like when seen but, because of its cryptic coloration and immobility, remaining

Camouflage is all-important to a roosting owl. This grey-phase Screech Owl shows its cryptically patterned plumage particularly well.

A Long-eared Owl on the alert, with ear-tufts erect, watching the photographer.

Two Scops Owls. Compare the relaxed pose of the young bird (left) with that of the adult (right) which has gone on the alert, stretching upright with the feathers held close in against the body.

completely inconspicuous. It is, of course, fully alert even when apparently asleep, and while the author has managed to creep to within a metre or two of a sleeping Golden Eagle and a dozing Raven, this would not be possible with an owl. On being disturbed, the owl not only tends to raise its ear-tufts but also to tighten its rather loose plumage so that quite suddenly what was once a relaxed and rather plump-looking owl becomes a surprisingly slim bird resembling a piece of bark or a short broken branch.

Not only birdwatchers find sleeping owls: other birds do so as they go about their daily business – usually accidentally. The shape of an owl is recognized instinctively by many small birds. To them it spells potential danger, or worse. Small birds' reaction to an owl is rather similar to that displayed when another predator is sighted, be it a hawk, a Weasel, or an ordinary domestic cat. The reaction is called **mobbing** and involves making as much noise as possible to advertise the predator's presence, to expose its whereabouts to other birds and animals, and hopefully to persuade it to move on. Mobbing is usually a noisy and actively demonstrative business and does not often involve actual attacks on the predator concerned although this does happen. The author has, for instance, seen a fox almost beaten to its knees by a gang of Rooks, and a Stoat actually bowled over by a furious Jackdaw.

Owls are seldom touched, it seems and, like most predators, they do not usually strike back at their tormentors. Indeed, retaliation by any predatory bird which is being mobbed is rather rare. Normally, it simply takes evasive action and, in the case of most birds of prey, simply outflies its pursuers. Owls often just sit there, seemingly undeterred by the frenzy of activity a mobbing is in progress but sometimes this may only reveal a place where an owl has been hiding away. Small birds remember owl roost sites and will sometimes become upset about them even when no owl is actually present.

Going back to the general plumage characteristics of owls, we find that in some species two distinct colour phases occur, which are not geographically separated. This difference in form between members of the same species is called dimorphism. It is seen particularly well

Owls may roost in a variety of places where they can enjoy peace and quiet; this Tawny Owl has chosen an old mill wheel.

around them, and hope that their disturbers will go away – which they eventually do, often conspicuously avoiding the area where the owl is sitting once they have given its position away. The mobbing activity has survival value for non-predatory birds whether the owl is a potential threat or not (and while it is roosting it is unlikely to be so), because they have drawn attention to it and are at least on the alert. For the owl, the matter probably only has nuisance value and not much more – though if things become too difficult it may well move away and find a quieter or better-concealed place. It is sometimes possible to find a roosting owl when in the North American screech owls, which have grey and rufous phases, and the Tawny Owl (curiously misnamed because it is not especially tawny in colour) also has a rather rare grey phase. This form of dimorphism is genetically based and, though precisely how and why such a permanent feature comes about is not fully understood, it presumably has some survival value in that it enables a species to adapt to a wide range of environmental conditions. Thus, the screech owls' grey phase is well adapted to a life in coniferous-type woodland, while the rufous phase is better suited to life among broadleaved trees. In the United States, as in a

53

Owls are habitually mobbed by small birds, but seldom actually attacked. This captive Great Horned Owl looks distinctly surprised when struck from behind by a Mockingbird.

number of other countries, timber production demands the widespread planting of commercially viable conifer crops, often at the expense of broadleaved (and often more 'natural') woodland. The rufous-phase screech owl moves out when its favoured woodland type is removed in this way but the species does not lose out because grey phase birds move in instead.

Another dimorphic feature, this time differentiating the sexes, occurs in many owls: this is not a plumage difference, such as we see in many birds, but a size difference. In common with many of the diurnal raptors, there is often a marked difference in the size and weight of the two sexes – in both cases the female being the larger. Although the difference is often obvious in owls, it does not quite reach the extremes seen in, for example, some of the sparrowhawks and goshawks where females may actually weigh twice as much as males. Generally, size differ-

ences between the sexes are most marked in those owls which feed mainly on vertebrate prey such as mammals and birds, and least obvious in principally insectivorous species; those which are more catholic in terms of the prey they eat fall somewhere between these two extremes. As with every generalization, this concerning size differences has its exceptions: the Burrowing Owl is one such, the male being slightly larger than the female.

A number of authorities have put forward different explanations for this back-to-front size dimorphism among birds of prey, but rather little work has been done on this difficult subject with regard to owls. One of the most commonly advanced theories suggests that a size difference allows a pair of birds to be as efficient as possible in exploiting the range of prey available to them, minimizing competition for the same food resources. A second explanation is linked to the nesting period. At this time, the male provides most of the food for the young while they are small and the female spends most of her time with them at the nest. Later on, when the chicks are more self-sufficient, the female begins hunting too, and is thought to bring in larger prey items which meet the increased food requirements of her rapidly growing family. There is some evidence to support both these theories among the diurnal birds of prey at least, although there is not a lot to show that males consistently take smaller prey than females, or vice-versa. There is even less evidence for these theories with the owls, partly because it is virtually impossible to determine which sex is responsible for producing the prey remains which allow us to find out something about the diets of the various species. It seems reasonable to suppose, however, that there is some degree of truth in both explanations; but they seem to be secondary to another, more complicated explanation which currently enjoys more support.

It is believed that rapacious birds which are by nature aggressive, and often rather solitary, may even regard others of the same species as potential prey. If this is so, it would at once pose difficulties for a pair of birds coming together, mating, and rearing a family. Nature has evolved a whole series of ritualized displays by which this basic aggressiveness is broken down and in which appeasement is an important factor. The male is the more dominant or 'aggressive' bird during courtship, and it is thought that the greater size of the female may counteract this, ensuring that she is able to stand on an equal footing with him, establishing an equilibrium between them. As a further development of this theme, it has also been suggested that the female's greater size may, in addition, provide protection for the young against possible predation by the male. There are various arguments for and against this general theory too, but it does seem as if the best explanation for this size disparity, both in owls and diurnal raptors, is an adaptation which has a survival value in that it helps in pair formation and the successful rearing of a family.

Moving on to consider the visible adaptations for the owl's way of life, we should look next at wings and how these are used. Most owls have relatively large, rounded wings which are rather short in those species which habitually hunt in cover, and much longer in those which hunt in open country or are strongly migratory. They have this much in common – their area is broad in comparison to the weight of the body or, in aeronautical terms, they have a low wing-loading. This enables them to fly very buoyantly and effortlessly, without too much flapping which would probably be rather noisy and would also use up a lot of energy. It enables them to glide easily, too, and to move about slowly for long periods at a time. Night hunting cannot be carried out at speed – a slow-moving, buoyant bird which is able to manoeuvre without effort

and to pause and hover easily (as some owls often do) will be far more successful than one which uses up a lot of energy rushing all over the place. In any case, the owl's vision and hearing are geared towards the careful approach, as we shall see.

Unfortunately, we are hardly ever able to watch owls actually hunting by night, or at best we can only catch short glimpses of them doing so. On particularly light nights, however, it is sometimes possible to see Barn Owls hunting, and these and some other species will also hunt in broad daylight when they have young to feed or in winter when they have to put in a lot of extra work to find enough food to stay alive. Then we can get some idea of how they work. A typically day-hunting bird like the Short-eared Owl provides even better opportunities for us to study how owl flight is used in hunting. The features which immediately catch

False eyes on the back of this Pearl-spotted Owlet's head are a warning sign to would-be predators approaching from behind.

55

the eye are the slow effortlessness of the birds, their ability to pause in mid-air for a better look or listen, and their very patient and methodical approach to the job on hand.

Any bird in flight makes a certain amount of noise through the very action of its wings moving through the air: this is very obvious with large birds or those like pheasants which have short, rounded wings and make a tremendous noise as they hurry away, but it is the case with small birds, too. Owls are a notable exception in this respect and it is one of the wonderful things about them that they are able to fly in utter silence – an owl flying past an observer at night suddenly appears from nowhere, without warning, and just as quickly is gone: there is no

feathers are 'hard' and smooth in appearance – which also helps reduce their resistance to the air through which they are passing. Owls have a sort of velvety pile over their wing-surface feathers and the edges of their flight feathers have soft fringes. These features damp down the sound of the air passing over and through the feathers to the extent that it is negligible. An owl sacrifices some flying efficiency because these very refinements produce more drag, or resistance to the air, but clearly these are unimportant sacrifices compared to the gains made through noiseless flight. These features are highly developed in the essentially nocturnal owls but are absent in those which operate mainly in daylight and also on the fishing owls'

A Tawny Owl coming in to land. The large wing area compared to the size of the bird's body helps it to fly buoyantly and effortlessly.

sound at all. To be able to go about their business unheard is obviously of great importance to the night-hunting owls. It means that small mammals and birds do not hear them coming, and are taken by surpise, but it also means that the owl's own highly developed hearing apparatus is not upset by .wing noise made by the bird itself. It is easy enough to test how this works: we all know that when we are listening hard for small sounds we stand motionless and even hold our breaths so as to give our ears the maximum opportunity to detect the noises we are investigating. That owls are able to do the same while still actively moving about is quite remarkable.

They achieve this by having certain modifications to their wing feathers. Most birds have no need to fly silently, so that their wing

wing feathers. Fishing owls have no need to fly silently to capture their particular prey which cannot hear them anyway.

Another more obvious structural feature is the development of owls' feet. Like the diurnal birds of prey, they use their feet to kill their prey as well as for perching, standing, and walking. To this end, they have relatively short, thick legs and strong toes armed with large, hooked talons. Some of the more terrestrial species, such as the Burrowing Owl, have rather longer legs better suited for walking.

Birds' feet, or more correctly their toes, are arranged in a number of different ways. Basically, they have four toes and in most perching birds three of these are directed forwards and the fourth backwards so that it functions rather like a thumb and enables the bird to grip.

A few swimming birds, such as the cormorants and the pelicans, have all four toes joined by webs, but most swimming species have only a rudimentary hind toe, as do most ground-dwelling birds. In both cases there is little need for an ability to perch and 'grasp'. Some specialists have evolved differently – for example, woodpeckers gain a really firm grip on tree trunks by having two toes facing forwards and two back.

In a sense, owls enjoy the best of both worlds. Their outer toe is actually reversible so that they can carry it in an orthodox position (though it often points sideways rather than to the front) or they can have two in front and two behind improving their ability to grip quite

possible bites by certain of their prey species, although it is interesting to note in passing that, while many diurnal birds of prey have feathered legs, their toes are naked. The Snowy Owl has exceptionally dense feathering on its legs and toes, providing extra insulation against the cold in arctic winters. Most other species found far to the north perch in trees rather than on the bare ground and use the thick, loose feathering of their lower underparts to cover their feet and keep them warm.

The fishing owls mostly lack the feathered legs of their cousins. Their prey is often rather slimy and their legs are often in water, so that in the interests of general cleanliness and keeping dry, bare legs are more useful to them. Like the

considerably. It is interesting that, among the diurnal raptors, only the Osprey shares this ability with the owls enabling it to gain a good grip on the slippery fishes which are its main prey.

Owls' feet have a wide spread which, with the reversible toe, allows them to seize their prey in the most efficient manner possible. In addition, they have exceptionally strong toes – necessary for piercing with their talons the vital parts of their prey, which is normally killed outright (unless it is very large) as soon as it is struck. Many an ornithologist who has handled owls can testify to the strength of an owl's grip and to the sharpness of its talons! Another curious feature, shared by almost all owls, is that their legs are feathered right down to the toes. This feathering has a protective function against

Osprey, they have a series of tiny, sharp projections known as **spicules** on the undersides of their toes – a special adaptation to help them grip their slippery prey.

Contrary to popular opinion, the beaks of birds of prey are not, as a rule, used for killing. Their primary function is to tear up prey. Owls share with the diurnal raptors a strongly hooked bill, varying in size and shape according to the species and the size and type of prey taken. The bills of the great eagle owls are comparable in size and strength to those of some of the largest diurnal raptors but, as with most owls, they are partly hidden by the feathering on the birds' faces. Two other features are worthy of mention. Firstly, the beaks of owls tend to be set rather lower and to curve down rather more steeply than those of most birds of prey so that they do

A Saw-whet Owl in flight showing the relatively short wings typical of owls which hunt in woodland.

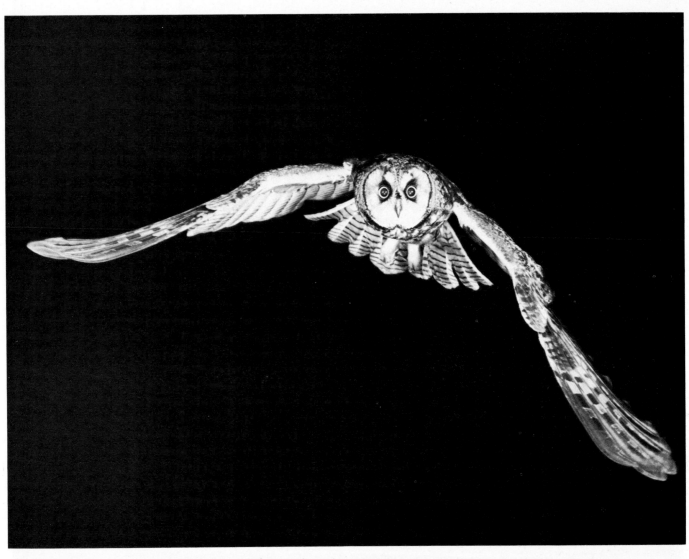

58

Far left top
A Long-eared Owl showing the longer wings of an owl which does most of its hunting in open country.

Far left bottom
The wing feathers of this Great Horned Owl have soft fringes and a covering of soft pile, enabling the bird to fly silently – important to it for taking its prey unawares and in the use of its own acute hearing.

Top left
The powerful toes and talons of an owl – its killing apparatus.

Top right
While most owls have feathered legs to protect them from bites from their prey species, the legs of the fishing owls are bare. Feathered legs are of no use in water and would soon be fouled by wet and slimy prey.

Bottom
A Barred Owl showing the powerful bill used for dismembering prey, and the immensely strong talons.

Even at this early age, a young Great Horned Owl's feet are large and powerful.

not interfere with the owl's field of vision from its forward-facing eyes. Secondly, the nostrils are set in a bare area at the base of the bill known as the **cere**. The cere is a feature shared with some other birds, including birds of prey, but its precise function is unknown. It is worth mentioning in passing that, in common with virtually all birds, owls have practically no sense of smell or, at best, it is probably very poorly developed. Sight and hearing are far more important to birds although one group, the kiwis, which are nocturnal feeders, have a highly developed sense of smell. The quite extraordinary lengths to which these two senses have developed in owls are easily the most remarkable of all their characteristics.

It is often said that owls can 'see in the dark' and while this is true in the broad sense it should not be interpreted too literally. In total darkness an owl can see no better than a man

but total darkness scarcely occurs in nature. There is always some light and owls have evolved so that they can make the maximum use of even the smallest amounts of it. This means that they see extremely well in 'natural darkness', even on the very darkest nights when we would be totally helpless. It has been said that their night vision is at least thirty-five times better than ours and that this is probably a considerable underestimate. Whatever the arithmetic, it is, by our standards, phenomenal.

Many people have also assumed, quite wrongly, that owls cannot see at all well in full daylight. In fact, they can probably see just as well as most other birds and no doubt share with many of them powers of daytime vision which are far superior to our own. It is obvious that owls which hunt partly or exclusively by day have exceptionally keen eyesight, but even the most nocturnal species are known to have

'twenty-four-hour vision' and can cope perfectly well in daylight. Barn Owls, for example, are known to be able to detect prey by sight on the darkest nights but anyone who has watched one hunting voles in a grass field on a bright winter's morning could testify that they are every bit as capable of finding their prey in exactly the opposite conditions.

Before we examine the special features which make the eyes of owls so efficient, we should look at the eye of a more orthodox bird and see how it works. Essentially, the eye is an organ which receives light and converts this into a message which is sent to the brain for analysis and interpretation. The light enters the eye through the cornea, a strong transparent covering on the eye's external face which in a sense functions rather like a window. This light then passes into the interior of the eye through the pupil. Around the pupil there is a coloured ring

(often yellow or orange in owls, for example, and various shades in our own eyes) known as the iris. This is muscular and by expansion and contraction controls the size of the pupil and, thus, the amount of light passing into the inner eye. In bright light the pupil is small but in poor light and, especially in darkness, it expands considerably. Just how this works can be seen by looking in a mirror and seeing what happens to your own eyes in different light conditions. It can also be seen particularly well in the eyes of a cat – the pupil is a mere slit of black in strong sunlight, but a quite different shape in duller light.

Once it has passed into the eye, the light passes through a thick, transparent lens, rather flat in appearance in most birds, which can be adjusted by muscles attached to it. The light is then focused on to the highly sensitive retina at the rear of the eyeball where it is converted into

The eyes of a Great Horned Owl are exceptionally sensitive organs with which the bird can see well on the darkest nights. The binocular vision helps to pinpoint prey with great accuracy.

impulses which travel to the brain via the optic
nerve. Analysis and interpretation of these
impulses is carried out in the visual cortex of the
brain.

In most birds, the eyeball is roughly spherical
– similar in shape to our own. The cornea is
relatively small and, indeed, the eyes of many
birds often strike us as remarkably small when
compared to the other dimensions of their heads.
The rather flat lens is relatively distant from
the retina at the back of the eye and projects a
large image upon it. This arrangement allows
the eye to function well in good light and to
achieve very good perception of detail or visual
acuity.

The degree of visual acuity depends on how
the light is dealt with when it falls on the retina.
In vertebrates, the group which includes birds
and men, there are two types of cells which
receive light, the cones and the rods, so called
from their approximate shapes. Cones are more
or less cylindrical in form and are only stimulated by high levels of light. They deal with
accurate perception and also with colour vision.
At levels where the cones are unable to function,
the rods take over.

Cones occupy a fairly central position on the retina, that is, they are in the direct path of the incoming light, while the rods tend to be situated more around the perimeter of the cone area. When this arrangement applies, as it does in diurnal birds, in which the number of cones present usually far outweighs the number of rods, it results in excellent day vision and visual acuity. Correspondingly, this arrangement leads to poor vision by night. We can again use our own eyes to test how this distribution of the receptor cells works. If we look directly at an object in darkness, we cannot see it particularly well, but if we look very slightly to one side of it there is an angle at which we can perceive it much more clearly as the rods lying to the side of the main cone area come into play.

In diurnal birds, then, cones predominate, and in some of them, notably some of the large eagles and vultures, further modifications in cone concentration give rise to incredible visual acuity which enables these birds to spot and identify even very small objects at a considerable distance. In nocturnal animals, it is the rods which predominate to give the best possible vision in darkness. This is the case with owls, as we might expect. Nevertheless, it is a curious fact that owls conform to this general rule but at the same time have managed to evolve eyes which retain considerable visual acuity – an asset which is often lost in other nocturnal creatures.

It can be seen at once from looking at the photographs in this book that owls have very large eyes – a feature common to other nocturnal birds but best shown in this order. It seems fairly obvious that the larger the eye, the more light it will admit and the better will be the owner's vision in dull conditions or in darkness. This is certainly the case with owls' eyes – which in the largest species are actually as big as our own – but it is not the whole story. Size alone is not enough to account for owls being able to 'see in the dark'; there are other very important modifications, too.

The cornea is relatively bigger than in most other birds, as is the lens. This arrangement allows as much light as possible to enter the inner eye but if this were to be resolved through the cells of the retina in the same way as in orthodox birds' eyes, the retina would have to be placed a very long way back from the lens for the job to be done efficiently. Rather than have a very elongated head to accommodate such a system, and to avoid the loss of light which would arise from throwing it back so far, owls have developed a much rounder lens which can focus the light over a shorter distance without loss of brightness. In fact, the eye chamber is relatively smaller than in most birds and the whole shape of the eyeball is noticeably tubular rather than spherical.

An owl's eye is, therefore, a highly sensitive organ which is fully operative in all its aspects during darkness. In daytime, it is protected by the iris closing the pupil considerably, so that only a little light is admitted. Quite enough light is still admitted, however, to provide excellent day vision, as we have said, and we have reason to believe that it is probably superior to our own. Additional protection is provided by a third eyelid, the **nictitating membrane**, which is transparent in many birds and has a generally protective function. Its opaqueness in the owls serves as a further barrier to the admission of too much light into the eye.

The large, basically tubular eyes possessed by owls occupy a large part of the bird's skull. In accommodating all this visual apparatus, owls have sacrificed virtually all the mobility of their eyeballs which is present in most birds to some degree and something which we take for granted. But here, too, owls have produced a compensatory development: they have exceptionally mobile necks to cope with the amount of head movement necessary to overcome having rigidly positioned eyes. If you walk up on an owl, it is quite extraordinary how the bird's head turns to follow every movement. An owl can look right over its shoulder when you pass behind it, without moving its body at all. We know that in some species at least the head can be rotated through 270 degrees.

Another very obvious feature of owls' eyes is that they are positioned side by side and face forwards, in much the same way as our own. Like us, owls enjoy binocular vision, that is, they look at an object with both eyes and in so doing can judge its position accurately. This is known as the parallax method and it works better the further apart the eyes are placed. Larger owls have their eyes well spaced, and it seems that the smaller species, by having rather flatter skulls, have developed as far as is physically reasonable to achieve similar spacing. Owls can further improve this three-dimensional vision by constantly moving and bobbing their heads so that each eye gets a number of sightings of the object under scrutiny from a variety of minutely different angles. The delightful head-bobbing movements of some of the smaller owls (which even includes turning the head fully upside-down on occasion) may be amusing but it is only the bird going through the process of assessing what it sees as fully as possible before deciding what action to take.

Binocular vision has developed to some degree in many predatory birds, including the diurnal birds of prey, herons and their allies, and various fish-catching seabirds. In the owls, binocular vision is possible through 70 degrees of their entire visual field of about 110 degrees, which is roughly half our own binocular field of 140 degrees out of a visual span of 180 degrees. More birds are among the 'hunted' than the 'hunters' and in their case all-round observation is very necessary in their constant watch for approaching predators. In a bird such as a pigeon, which has its eyes on the sides of its head, the total visual field is some 340 degrees, with only about 20 degrees of binocular vision to the front. It has a 'blind spot' to its rear, which it

covers by moving its head, but even this is obviated in Woodcocks in which the eyes are set rather further back than in most birds so that they can actually see all round at once, with small areas of binocular overlap to both front and rear. The advantages of having a wide field of binocular vision if you are a predatory bird can again be tested easily by using your own eyes. See how well you can judge distances with one eye fully covered compared with using the normal two.

A number of experiments has been carried out under laboratory conditions, notably with Barn Owls in the United States, to discover just how well owls' eyes work and to what extent they can see in the dark. We need not go into the details here but the experiments have shown beyond any doubt that owls can operate success-fully in conditions where a man cannot see at all. Leading on from this, it has also been demon-strated with some owl species that they can actually catch prey, provided it is alive and moving, even in total darkness. Other animals have incredible systems akin to radar for hunting and avoiding obstacles in total darkness. Bats are the best-known exponents of this type of 'flying blind', but among birds it is also practised by the curious oilbirds, cousins of the nightjars and, thus, probably related to owls, too. But owls do not use anything quite so sophisticated as echo location. Instead, they rely on a hearing system which is every bit as remarkable as their night vision.

Birds do not possess externally visible ears, which are so characteristic a feature of most mammals including man, so that there are many misconceptions about their hearing. Actually, birds have, for the most part, exceptionally acute hearing. It is an essential sense to them in survival terms, whether for locating their prey or gaining early warning of the approach of their predators. Therefore, owls are not alone in having well-developed auditory organs, but they are unique among birds in the degree to which their hearing has developed. It is probably true to say that among many species it is every bit as important to them as hunters as their extraordinary eyesight. It is not generally real-ized that nocturnal owls hunt by ear as much as by sight.

As we would expect, the maximum evolution towards the ultimate in hearing has occurred among the nocturnal owls. These possess the largest and most sensitive ears. It has also been pointed out that the developments are apparently more marked among temperate and subarctic species than tropical ones, perhaps because the cacophony of sound often present in tropical forests militates against too much use of the ears alone. Northern woods are generally much quieter places by night. It would be a mistake, however, to assume that diurnal owls do not use their ears when hunting. Very often their prey, such as small mammals, may be concealed in long grass or other vegetation and may be located by sound as much as by sight. It seems that this is the case, too, with some of the diurnal raptors. The harriers are a case in point. To some extent these long-winged, buoyantly flying hawks resemble the Short-eared Owl and its close cousins in the way they slowly patrol over grasslands, looking and listening. Further evidence is provided by the fact that they also possess quite well-developed facial discs, so that they resemble owls superficially. As we have already said, facial discs are connected with hearing, in spite of the fact that they are positioned around the eyes.

It has not yet been established precisely how facial discs improve the reception of sound into an owl's ears. They do not function quite like the parabolic reflectors they resemble, which concentrate sound to the front, but somehow they do help to funnel sound waves into the owl's ears which lie directly behind them. Facial discs are highly developed in the more nocturnal owls, especially the species with a less tropical distribution, and are ill-defined or virtually absent in some species in which hearing does not seem to play a very important role in hunting.

Members of highly nocturnal genera like *Strix*, *Asio*, *Tyto*, and others have surprisingly huge, half-moon-shaped ear openings im-mediately behind the rear edges of their facial discs, so long that they seem to produce narrow openings in the head extending from crown to neck. They are truly enormous for the size of the head which carries them, so that the inevitable comment that owls' heads are largely full of eyes and ears is not so far removed from the truth.

There are long, very mobile flaps fringing the ear openings to the front and the rear which can open and close the aperture and change its

64

The two colour phases of the Screech Owl: red phase on the left, grey on the right.

A ground-dwelling owl with long legs – the Burrowing Owl from North and Central America.

shape at will so that an owl can concentrate on sounds coming from any quarter. The mobility of these ear-flaps also affects the shape of the facial discs – which can be seen to be mobile when a dozing owl is disturbed. If we return again to our roosting Long-eared Owl (a species with highly developed hearing) we can often see that its facial discs are 'closed' when it is sitting peacefully – giving the bird an oddly un-owl-like expression at times. Once the owl is aware that someone is nearby and becomes alert, the facial discs slowly open as the ears come into full use – and an owl-like expression quickly results. When this species is abroad and hunting by night, its facial appearance is quite different to that which we often see in roosting birds. This feature, which is well seen in photographs of this species, might at first suggest two quite different owl species, which can often be a source of considerable confusion until we realize that many owls, unlike other birds, have exceptionally mobile 'faces'.

The nocturnal owls can detect extremely small sounds, such as may often be made by

A Great Horned
Owl showing the
nictitating membrane
or third eyelid which
protects the sensitive
eyes.

A Barn Owl, which
is blind in one eye.
The loss of an eye no
doubt reduces
hunting efficiency,
but many one-eyed
owls seem to live
quite successfully
with this handicap.

A Tawny Owl in flight. Note the rather short, broad, and rounded wings of this woodland hunter.

Wings spread and thrust forward to function as brakes, a Screech Owl touches down.

The facial discs on this Barn Owl are half closed. These discs are highly mobile and help to channel sounds into the large and very sensitive ears which lie behind them.

small, furtive prey animals at large by night, which cannot be detected by human ears. Nor do they need constant repetition of these sounds to enable them to locate and then capture their prey. In the experiments mentioned above, when it was shown that capture was possible in conditions when even owls could not see, it was found that one tiny sound was enough for the owl to roughly locate the source and only one more was necessary to place it precisely. The owl was then able to strike with precision.

By moving their heads around and adjusting their ears as described, owls can locate prey very accurately indeed – the principle being not too different to that adopted when getting a visual fix on an object by looking at it from a variety of different angles. But owls have refined their techniques still further by possessing, in some species, asymmetrical ears. One ear is much larger than the other (as much as 50 per cent bigger in some species) and in addition is usually placed higher on the side of the head than the other – the right ear usually being the larger and higher. This curious arrangement vastly improves the range of 'fixes' an owl can make on a sound, and by moving its head around until the sound registers equally in both ears it will actually end up facing its prey – which is of

A Screech Owl on the alert – with its feathers pressed close to its body, it seems a fragile little bird, but notice the powerful feet and the broad head housing the large eyes and ears.

obvious advantage when the prey cannot be seen. Any movement out of line on the part of the prey animal is immediately detected, and using its finely tuned hearing apparatus the owl is able to adjust back to the correct line very quickly indeed. On setting out to capture unseen prey, the owl homes in on it head first, as has been shown by photographing Barn Owls striking in total darkness in laboratory conditions using infra-red photography techniques. The minute adjustments necessary to bring the head into line again should the prey move can even be made in flight as the owl swings down, gently flapping, towards the source of the sound.

Only at the very last minute is the head thrown back out of the way so that the talons can be flung forwards for the actual kill. If an owl is capable of this sort of incredible accuracy in total darkness, it can be seen quite easily that in more normal conditions at night the combination of this exceptional hearing ability and the equally remarkable night vision of the bird produces a predator which is truly a master of its element.

Having summarized the unique aspects of the owl physique, we shall in the following chapters see how these relate to the bird's way of life in terms of hunting and prey relations and of the life cycle of some owl species.

69

Owls and their prey

You have seen how owls are specially adapted to living and hunting at night, so that we now move on to consider how they make use of their special skills in hunting and killing, what they eat, and how they live in balance with their food supply. Before going any further, however, it is essential to look at the question of predation in general terms and clear away some of the misconceptions which surround what is often a highly emotive subject.

At the outset, we should see the role of owls in its true perspective. Owls form but one small part of the immense and intricate web of life in which, if we strip things down to bare essentials, there is a complex interrelationship between all living things as they feed upon one another. Owls are one kind of a whole host of predators which exist by eating other living creatures. Distasteful as predation may seem to some of us, it is not wrong, or immoral, or even unusual, all of which are labels which have been attached to it. Owls kill merely to feed themselves and their offspring – there is no wholesale slaughter, as some believe, because they only kill what they require to eat. They do not kill wantonly or for pleasure, but only from necessity. They are highly skilled and extremely efficient killers and there is certainly no cruelty involved.

Cruelty is a human concept generally applied only to human activities and an owl killing a small bird or a mouse is no more cruel than a spider catching a fly, or a Blackbird pulling a worm out of the lawn.

Unfortunately, the role of the predator is often misunderstood and equally often sensationalized and grossly misrepresented, leading in turn to a whole range of feelings on our part which range from mild dislike through to hatred; the latter will often lead to merciless persecution. Moral considerations apart, predatory birds are disliked and killed in their turn because it is thought that they decrease the numbers of the animals upon which they feed, or even exterminate them – or, in other words, that they exert a controlling influence over their prey. While this can, indeed, be the case in certain limited and usually very temporary circumstances, the reverse situation actually applies. The numbers of predators are limited by the numbers and availability of their prey and, in addition, the animals killed by predators are part of a surplus of individuals which is produced in a wild population and which would perish anyway in the long term whether predated or not. It is only when man introduces highly artificial situations into natural populations that

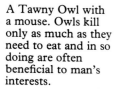

A Tawny Owl with a mouse. Owls kill only as much as they need to eat and in so doing are often beneficial to man's interests.

70

The kill: this Saw-whet Owl throws both feet upwards and forwards as it strikes.

the finely balanced relationships between predators and prey sometimes go awry. The basic laws of nature with regard to hunters and hunted are particularly well demonstrated by the interrelationships of owls and their prey, as we shall see.

The question of man's relationships with owls is discussed more fully at the end of this book, but in passing we should perhaps comment on one important practical consideration. One way of evaluating wildlife (a selfish one in the eyes of some people) is to ask whether it is advantageous to us in practical or economic terms. It is highly doubtful whether any owl is harmful to man's interests and very likely that many of those which live in close contact with him are actually beneficial — that highly effective rat-catcher the Barn Owl, for example — while most owls are at least 'neutral' in this respect.

From our earlier survey of the various owl genera, you can see that they are a fairly close-knit group of birds, conforming to much the same general physical pattern of non-specialist predators and most highly developed towards living in the dark. Like the hawks, falcons, and their allies, they usually kill by striking and grasping with their strongly hooked talons, using their bills in some cases to administer a *coup de grâce* but otherwise only to deal with their prey once it has been killed. If you are ever given a live owl to hold (or any of the diurnal raptors either) you have little to fear from its beak, however dangerous a weapon it may look:

the feet and talons are the things to avoid.

Unlike the day-hunting raptors, owls have relatively few techniques which they use to hunt and kill their prey. Essentially, owls employ two basic methods, both of which are common to the majority of diurnal birds of prey also. The first and probably more widely practised method is the tactic of watching, listening, and waiting. Owls use a variety of perches as vantage points when searching for their prey, depending entirely on what is available in their particular habitat — rocks, hummocks, fence posts, telegraph poles, and a variety of man-made perches are used just as readily as live or dead trees, bushes, or other vegetation. From these they make their kill with a short, direct pounce when a likely item of prey has been located. They will move from one perch to another while hunting and, because most owls are opportunist hunters, may well strike from the air while doing so or, with some species, pause to hover as they go along. Hovering is a technique practised by various birds of prey, usually those which hunt in more open country, and among the owls is widely used by Barn and Hawk Owls. In effect it simply provides an aerial perch for the bird so that its effect is only slightly different from actually pitching somewhere for a look round. The prey captured when using any of these 'waiting and watching' tactics is most often on the ground — most mammals and insects are probably secured there — but sallies will also be made after flying insects and, among the

Far left
The Great Grey Owl
has large facial discs
and surprisingly
small eyes; it often
hunts by day.

Left
A Long-eared Owl
incubating, showing
the long ear-tufts
particularly well;
these are depressed
when the bird is
relaxed.

diurnal owls, after passing birds, too. Flying birds are normally only taken when they can be surprised and grabbed quickly and only a few owls are capable of more active or sustained pursuit in flight – no owl can match the expertise of some of the small hawks and many of the falcons in this respect. Similarly, not many owls are particularly proficient at chasing and capturing night-flying insects – other nocturnal hunters have cornered this particular market, notably many species of bats and, among birds, those specialist insectivores the nightjars and their close cousins.

Opportunist hunting almost occupies a position between the two main methods. On their nightly travels, owls may encounter all sorts of creatures they can kill, both those which are abroad by night and those which are asleep, and they will then act accordingly. Thus, almost any roosting bird which an owl can reach may fall prey to the passing predator and indeed we know that regular roost sites will be visited night after night by some species of owls. This, then, becomes deliberate rather than merely opportunist hunting. When very large owls are in the neighbourhood, even their smaller cousins are not immune from attack. Eurasian Eagle Owls, for example, kill many Long-eared Owls as well as other species, and have even been recorded as taking the Snowy Owl, a species almost as big and powerful as they are themselves. In southern Europe, the Tawny Owl is listed as a predator of the little Scops Owl, and it has even been

Above
Prey may be carried in the bill, as in the case of this moth brought in by a Little Owl.

Right
Prey may also be carried in the feet, as with this Pygmy Owl with a small rodent.

suggested that in some areas it has caused a partial decline in the population of the smaller bird. Nor are other birds of prey ignored. Among the prey taken by eagle owls in Europe and in America there is a striking list of species, even up to the size of buzzards and Goshawks.

Bats have featured in the prey remains of a number of owls but because no owl has evolved anything approaching the highly specialized techniques of the twilight-hunting Bat Hawk, nor the supreme speed and agility of other bat-catchers such as the hobbies, it is unlikely that many bats are caught on the wing. The more likely explanation is that bats are captured while they are at rest or are emerging from their roosts – when they are singularly helpless – or, in the case of tropical fruit-eating bats, while they are actually feeding.

Turning to the second main method of hunting, namely hunting in flight, we find that this is the province of the longer-winged owls of open country, of which the Short-eared Owl is a notable example. Some owls, such as the Barn Owl, can use both methods of hunting. It will patrol hedgerows and roadside verges either by flying along slowly and very deliberately, alternately gliding and flapping, and also by using any convenient perch along the way, or it will just as readily quarter the adjoining fields for long periods at a time without landing. The capture of prey located by a slow-flying owl is again made by a short, swift, direct pounce, and

is seldom made from any great height.

However they are hunting, owls are not successful every time they strike at prey – which is equally true of all birds of prey. Sometimes, though, there may be a second chance if the owl misses at the first attempt. The author has seen Short-eared and Barn Owls chase prey on foot which they have missed from an aerial strike, and has also seen the former species chase missed birds in the air with quite remarkable speed and dexterity over short distances.

Many owls use 'watch and wait' tactics and hunt from a perch, like this Pygmy Owl which has killed in this way.

75

Many owls feed on invertebrates and insects. At this nest site we see a Boobook Owl bringing in a centipede.

It is no accident that many of the owls we actually see are encountered along roads, either flapping along over the roadside or watching intently from a gate post or similar vantage point. Roads and their edges provide ideal open habitat where small prey becomes more visible and more vulnerable, and woodland owls will make just as much use of these 'corridors' through their domains as their cousins in open country. It is, however, an unfortunate fact that many owls

perish through this habit of frequenting roads. Traffic casualties occur all too often and Barn Owls seem to suffer particularly in this respect. They are a common sight along busy roads at night and the author has found as many as five killed by traffic along a single 50-kilometre (30-mile) stretch of a main road in England.

Some owls use other tactics in securing their prey. Both Little and Burrowing Owls, for example, will hunt successfully on foot and the

Oriental Hawk Owl has been seen apparently stalking crabs on foot on the shore in parts of south-east Asia. The Tawny Owl, a very versatile species, will sometimes take fishes from the surface of water and has even on occasion robbed goldfish ponds in gardens but, of course, the various fishing owls are the true specialists. Surprisingly, rather little is known about their feeding habits, especially the African species, but observations on some of those found in Asia

suggest that they all use suitable perches over-looking water and swoop down to lift fishes from the surface with their talons. As far as we know they do not actually plunge right into the water after fishes in the manner of an Osprey. Blakiston's Fish Owl at least fishes on foot by wading in the shallows in search of its prey and it seems very likely that this method may be used by other fishing owls, too.

As we have already said, scavenging and

Here, the Boobook Owl has caught a dragonfly.

77

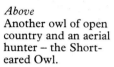

Above
Another owl of open country and an aerial hunter – the Short-eared Owl.

Above right
Snowy Owls hunt over open country and do so from the air.

Right
An exposed perch is often used as a look-out post by the day-hunting Hawk Owl.

carrion feeding do not enter very much into the owl's way of life, although the author's own observation of a Tawny Owl feeding on carrion might possibly suggest that some owls turn to this source of food on occasion. Some of the fishing owls have been seen scavenging along rivers, and both they and the Indian Forest Eagle Owl have been seen feeding on dead animals, including crocodile in the case of the former, and tiger in the latter! Some birds, notably the piratical skuas and some of the diurnal birds of prey, make a successful living through kleptoparasitism – the art of stealing prey caught by another. This habit does not

seem to have been recorded at all widely among owls, but in his book on African birds of prey, Leslie Brown quotes an instance of a Pearl-spotted Owlet knocking down a Wood-hoopoe in a surprise attack and stealing its beakful of food.

We know quite a lot about how owls locate and capture their prey, but what do we know about the actual make-up of their diets? Unfortunately, we come back to the familiar statement that very little is known in the case of a great many species, especially those with a tropical distribution and those found only on isolated islands. A few species have been studied in depth in the temperate Old and New Worlds, however, enabling us to build up a good picture of what they eat, how their food can vary from season to season, and how the numbers and availability of their prey influence their own numbers and breeding success.

You will readily appreciate that finding out about owls' prey by direct observation of hunting birds is exceptionally difficult – as indeed it is even with the diurnal birds of prey – and with many species, obtaining any meaningful data in this way is virtually impossible. To some extent, long-term studies of owls at the nest can provide much valuable information where the prey brought in and food remains left around can be identified, but here too there are snags. Such observations will only cover a relatively small part of an owl's year and in any case may not reveal very much about the diet of the adult birds. Equally, there are often difficulties in identifying prey, especially with insectivorous species. Most of the work which has been done so far has concentrated on the study of owl pellets, which are available in quantity all through the year. In an ideal study, pellet analysis plus detailed observations at a nest would provide most of the answers.

Except for the very largest items, owls usually swallow their prey whole, unlike the diurnal raptors, which tend to dismember it and swallow selected parts. In owls, the process of sorting out what is nourishing and what is not takes place internally. As soon as the owl's powerful stomach juices have extracted the matter which can be assimilated, the remaining 'hard parts' are

Some owls may hunt
on foot – Little Owls
do so regularly and
catch many earth-
worms in this way.

compressed into pellets and ejected via the mouth. These contain the teeth, bones, and fur of mammals, the bones, beaks, and feathers of birds, fragments of the external armour of insects, and even identifiable remains from worms and other invertebrates. With practice and patience, these pellets can be dissected and their components identified, providing a good record of what an owl has been eating.

Pellets are all roughly the same shape, rather like short sausages, but vary a great deal in size, texture, and colour according to the species producing them and what they contain. General- ly speaking, the largest owls produce the largest pellets. To the practised eye, the species of owl which produced the pellet can be ascertained without a bird ever being seen and it is some- times possible, at a glance, to get a good general impression of the sort of food remains it con- tains. Fortunately for the students of owls, the birds are very much creatures of habit and tend to deposit their pellets at roosts or other frequently used spots so that considerable quantities may accumulate. While this book was being written, the author's brother found Barn Owl pellets almost ankle deep in a cathedral tower where the birds had presumably been roosting and breeding for many years.

Unlike many diurnal birds of prey, owls usually swallow their prey whole. The indigestible parts are then ejected via the mouth as a tightly compressed pellet.

A Tawny Owl bringing prey to its nest site. Some of the first detailed studies of owls and their prey were carried out on this species.

The amateur naturalist can derive a great deal of pleasure and also produce useful information from dissecting pellets. They can be taken apart in their dry state, but it is usually better to soak them in warm water to separate the dried fur or feathers from the other remains, placing each individual item on clean blotting paper for examination. Mammals can usually be identified quite easily from their skulls, jaws, and teeth, and several of the better books on mammals contain useful sections on skulls and dentition (which are often vital clues in the identification of some small mammals). Birds' beaks provide helpful clues to their identity, as do their skulls (but these may not always be intact) and their pelvic girdles. Some help from experienced workers or a museum may be necessary for precise identification of some

species, and will also be very useful with the rather more difficult remains of insects and invertebrates. A microscope will obviously be a great help, but for most owl pellet work a good hand-lens is usually sufficient.

It should not be forgotten that it is not only the ornithologist who can benefit from examining owl pellets. What we find in them can sometimes produce very useful information on the numbers and distribution of the prey animals themselves. Small mammals in particular are difficult subjects to study and any sample of their population will be welcome to the mammalogist: owl pellets provide a ready-made sample and may be eagerly sought after!

While the remains found in pellets will tell us the numbers of the various prey species taken by owls, we must go a little further than

81

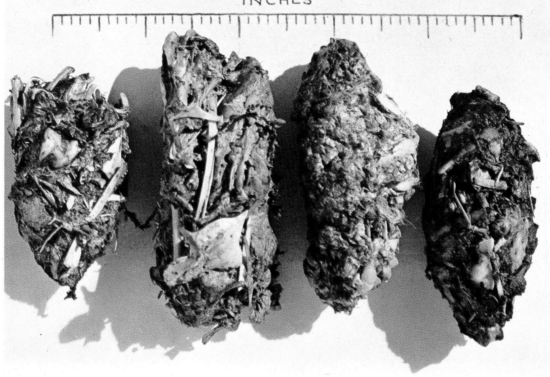

Snowy Owl pellets (above) and Long-eared Owl pellets (below). From a study of the indigestible prey remains in these pellets much can be learned about the diet of the birds.

CENTIMETRES

The Little Owl is a small species which kills many insects as well as rodents and small birds.

purely numerical recording and consider the food value of the various items. The basis for doing this – still widely used – was first suggested by Dr HN Southern in a classic study on Tawny Owls and their prey carried out some years ago in a large area of woodland near Oxford, England. This particular study remains the model on which many subsequent investigations have been based.

Dr Southern's work involved detailed observations at the nests of thirty pairs of owls and extensive pellet analysis. He found that these Tawny Owls fed mainly on small rodents and used one weighing 20 grams (0·7 ounce) (for example, mice and the smaller voles) as his 'standard rodent' equivalent to 'one prey unit'. Because they are smaller and weigh much less, Pygmy and Common Shrews needed five and

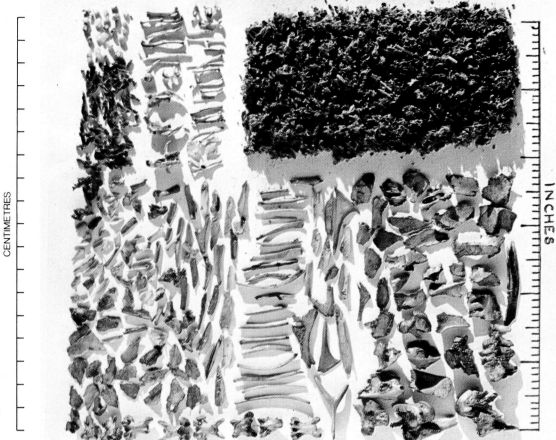

Dissected pellets of a Snowy Owl showing the bones of many small mammals.

CENTIMETRES

INCHES

The Short-eared Owl is a diurnal hunter, quartering open country in search of the voles which are its main prey.

84

two individuals respectively to make up one prey unit, while larger animals such as Moles and Brown Rats would be equivalent to five prey units. Therefore, using this system, we can deduce that while an animal like the Brown Rat may not be particularly numerous in terms of the numbers of individuals represented in prey remains, its food value to the owl may be quite high. For example, in a study of Long-eared Owls carried out in Ireland, rats made up only 5 per cent of the prey remains found in pellets, but using the conversion system devised during the Oxford study they represented about 20 per cent by weight of the food the owls were eating.

In the Oxford study it was found that the highly nocturnal Wood Mouse and the Bank Vole, a species which is much more active throughout the whole of a twenty-four-hour period, together made up about 60 per cent of the owls' prey. Various other small mammals, including Moles and young Rabbits, made up most of the balance, with beetles especially predominating among the remaining prey items. It was also seen that from December through to April, the principal food species were Wood Mice and Bank Voles, plus a certain number of Short-tailed Voles, but that from May, when the young owls would be about half grown, pellet contents showed a proportionate decrease in the numbers of voles and mice and an increase in the numbers of Moles and beetles, especially cockchafers. Observations at nests provided even more evidence of this seasonal change and also indicated that the food of the young might differ from that eaten by the adults themselves. Therefore, it became clear that to achieve a full picture of what the owls were eating as a family, both studies at the nest and the continuing analysis of pellet remains were essential.

The seasonal change also reflects a change in the owls' ability to catch the small mammals present on the woodland floor: from the spring onwards, the growth of vegetation renders these small animals harder to find and capture, so that some change in diet would be necessary. Another interesting feature in the Oxford study was that Moles – caught on the surface – were mainly young animals, and also that they were not brought to the nest at night, indicating that the Tawny Owls were also hunting in daylight.

A broadly similar choice of diet might be expected with any Tawny Owls which have their main home range in woodland, with differences in actual prey species according to the region, but where the habitat is markedly different, a versatile species like the Tawny Owl would be expected to adapt accordingly. Such is the case where this species occurs in towns and cities, where small mammals are usually less abundant and less important as prey. Birds often assume a greater importance to town dwellers, especially the ubiquitous House Sparrow which is regularly taken at roosts.

The Long-eared Owl, too, is primarily a rodent eater. It hunts not only in fairly closed woodland conditions, but also on all sorts of open ground adjacent to forests, thickets, and scrub, or even the small and rather narrow belts of trees where it sometimes nests. Like the Tawny Owl it is essentially a nocturnal hunter, though it, too, may appear well before darkness falls when it is feeding young, but it is a longer-winged species probably tending to hunt more in flight than from a perch.

In the Irish study mentioned above, Wood Mice formed about 70 per cent of the birds' prey by weight and were by far the most numerous individual species in terms of prey remains. Brown Rats, which would have been taken in much more open situations than the mice, were the next most important item at 20 per cent, while House Mice and small numbers of birds more or less equally accounted for the remaining 10 per cent. Another study, this time carried out in the Scottish Highlands in an area where pine forest adjoins moorland and other generally open areas, showed that the birds here were hunting more in the open. More than 80 per cent of the prey identified (again by weight) was small rodents, with the Short-tailed Vole at 54 per cent being the most numerous item, and the Wood Mouse scoring 21 per cent – the figures here referring to March, which is essentially still very much a winter month in that part of Scotland. By autumn, the numbers of Wood Mice taken had dropped considerably to a mere 3 per cent and the Bank Vole (14 per cent) had become a significant prey item. Short-tailed Voles were still important at 48 per cent indicating that this particular rodent is probably an important prey species throughout the year. These findings follow closely the results of similar studies made in Scandinavia.

Long-eared Owls often roost communally in winter, and sometimes in fairly close proximity to large roosts of small birds. Where they have been studied in such situations it seems that they may take a somewhat greater proportion of birds than is usually the case – and will patrol and raid roosts with great regularity – but even so rodents will still form the mainstay of their diet.

The Short-eared Owl is very closely related to the Long-eared but is much more a bird of open country, nesting on the ground and, as we have seen, hunting regularly in full daylight. It is hardly surprising to find that in many parts of Europe it preys, to a large extent, on the commonest small rodent of open country, the Short-tailed Vole. Where this vole does not occur, however, the owl will readily turn its attentions to other species. The same will happen where there are seasonal fluctuations in the abundance of the vole. In an area in the Outer Hebrides, Short-eared Owls were found to be feeding on a large proportion of voles (63 per cent of their diet by weight) between April and September, but also catching many Brown Rats, too (31 per cent). The Brown Rat is indeed an

important prey species to this owl in parts of Ireland, some of the Western Isles, and the Isle of Man where Short-tailed Voles or Common Shrews may be absent, and there is evidence to suggest that many are also eaten in agricultural areas of eastern England and also in coastal areas.

No-one who has watched a Short-eared Owl hunting a coastal marsh in winter can doubt that this species is also a proficient bird catcher. It gives the impression of moving rather slowly as it ceaselessly quarters the ground, swinging this way and that as it searches for prey, but in fact it has a surprisingly high air speed and this becomes very apparent when it suddenly swerves after a flock of small birds which it has disturbed or gives chase to small wading birds flushed from a creek or pool. Wintering owls in coastal habitats and those passing through on migration may well switch their diet to one which is dominated by birds, especially finches, pipits, larks, and the like, and also various wader species.

One of the most efficient of all the hunters of rats and mice is the Barn Owl, a species with feeding habits that are very definitely beneficial to man. Analysing close to 50000 individual prey items collected throughout Britain and Ireland, David Glue of the British Trust for Ornithology has shown that this species feeds almost exclusively on small rodents: shrews, mice, rats, and voles account for 90 per cent of all vertebrate prey eaten by British and Irish Barn Owls.

Many Barn Owls hunt mostly over rough

Above
Short-eared Owls eat mainly voles. This bird of the Galápagos race will also take young seabirds and small reptiles.

Right
Many small owls, like this Screech Owl, eat large numbers of insects.

The tiny Pygmy Owl is a formidable killer of small mammals and birds which may be as large as the owl itself.

grassland and in other very open habitats, including young forestry plantations, areas of scrub and marshland and its fringes, and here again we find the unfortunate Short-tailed Vole figuring as the owl's primary prey species. There is some regional and seasonal variation, and this vole is also subject to considerable population fluctuations, but as a general rule this is the main prey species. Common Shrews, Wood Mice (which are not found exclusively inside woodlands, where Barn Owls do not often hunt), and Brown Rats are the secondary prey species, and any one of these may assume particular importance where voles are scarce or absent altogether. Where the author lives, on the edge of the fen country, the Barn Owl is a fairly common species and is very often seen along roadsides and in association with the many ditches and small dykes which drain the flat agricultural countryside of the region. Here, the Brown Rat is a commonly seen and clearly very numerous rodent and there seems little doubt that fenland Barn Owls treat it as a major food source. In Ireland and the Isle of Man where Short-tailed Voles and Common Shrews are absent, the Brown Rat again becomes an important prey species, along with the Wood Mouse, and more House Mice and small birds are eaten than is normally the case. Most Barn Owls eat some birds, usually those with com-

munal roosts, and at times some may rely quite a lot on this type of prey, but taking the situation as a whole we find that this owl is not a major bird killer: only about 2 per cent of its prey is avian.

The Finnish ornithologists, Heimo Mikkola and Seppo Sulkava, have looked into the prey of the Great Grey Owl in Sweden and Finland, assessing the results of studies in both countries where prey remains were examined from a total of forty-two breeding sites and in addition looking at the stomach contents of forty-six dead owls outside the breeding season. This big owl of the northern spruce and pine forests would seem, by virtue of its great size and awesome aspect, to be a particularly powerful predator, but it was found that well over 90 per cent of their prey during the breeding season consisted of small voles. The Short-tailed Vole again features as a firm favourite, accounting for two-thirds of the total prey remains, with over a quarter made up of other vole species. About six species of shrew were the only other significant animals' remains found, though a few frogs and birds, as well as a few mammals other than small rodents, were also found. In view of its marked preference for very small prey, it is interesting to note that these others included some much larger creatures – the Red Squirrel in Sweden and birds as large as Hazel Hens and

87

Barn Owls kill many rats and mice, but many take young and full-grown birds, too.

Despite its great size, the Great Grey Owl preys almost entirely on small rodents. Its numbers and distribution are closely linked with the abundance of its prey.

Jays. No doubt this owl is presented with occasional opportunities to take a variety of prey, as are most owls, and acts accordingly. The stomach analyses from twenty-seven of the specimens examined (the other nineteen contained no remains) showed that small mammals were still the chief source of food outside the nesting season, although there was apparently a marked swing towards shrews (43 per cent) at the expense of voles (56 per cent), but this is largely accounted for by a decrease in vole numbers around the time the specimens were collected and the owls turning much more towards shrews as prey.

Another northern owl which has been studied in Europe (Norway, Finland, and Russia) is the

A large and powerful species, the Great Horned Owl is easily capable of tackling full-grown rabbits. Here, a female brings half a rabbit to the nest.

Hawk Owl, a largely diurnal species found in more open country with scattered trees and scrub in the boreal forest zone. There is some regional variation in prey preferences but, taking all three countries together, breeding birds were found to feed almost entirely (95 to 98 per cent of remains from nest sites) on voles. Only a few shrews, mice, frogs, and birds were recorded, but the last included species as big as the Willow Grouse. Once again, stomach remains were examined to find out what these owls eat in winter and these showed that the vole content dropped to 41 per cent while the bird content rose to nearly one-third. Here, too, the timing was such that vole populations were at one of their periodic low levels, but equally snow cover would have rendered mammal catching difficult for the owls and they had clearly switched to other more visible prey. It is interesting to note that the Willow Grouse seemed a firm favourite of these Hawk Owls – interesting because the Willow Grouse is very roughly the same size as a Hawk Owl and would seem a rather unlikely quarry, at least on a regular basis.

The Eurasian Eagle Owl is undoubtedly one

of the most versatile of all owls, an opportunist hunter capable of killing an extremely wide range of other animals and birds of all shapes and sizes. Studies have shown various prey preferences in different regions, and have also indicated some of the more unusual items of prey which may be taken. These are probably not particularly important in terms of food intake, even if the larger creatures will obviously feed an owl very well, but they do serve to show just how versatile these great owls can be – and how powerful. The list includes cats, dogs, full-grown foxes, and even adult Roe Deer!

In western Norway, mainly in areas at or near the coast, the Norwegian ornithologist, Johann Willgohs, has made an extensive study of Eagle Owls. In this region, mammals make up about 16 per cent of their prey intake by weight, with small rodents predominating. Among them, the Short-tailed Vole figures yet again as an important species, as does the Brown Rat – the owls preying extensively on the latter where they appear in large numbers around rubbish tips. Some lemmings are also eaten, but not in great quantities, and there is nothing to suggest that this little animal, with its greatly fluctuating

populations, is particularly important to Eagle Owls in the way that it is to some other northern owls and other birds of prey. A much larger animal, the Blue or Arctic Hare, which is an important prey species to some Eagle Owl populations, does not feature very often on the menu of the western Norwegian birds and is mostly recorded from sites inland rather than near the coast. A variety of other mammals is recorded by Dr Willgohs, including Hedgehogs (their spiny coats clearly hold no terrors for the big owls), Red Squirrels, and, among the smaller carnivores, escaped Mink, young Red Foxes, and domestic cats. Sheep are numerous and wide-spread in this region but only a handful of young lambs were found among prey remains; there was no evidence to show conclusively that Eagle Owls definitely kill lambs, in fact, and even if they do it must be a rare occurrence.

Birds are the major souce of food to this owl population – nearly two-thirds of the items recorded in prey remains were avian, accounting for something like 83 per cent of the owls' diet by weight. Seabirds made up almost half the total, being taken by the owls at and around their breeding areas by night, with the Common Gull, the Eider Duck, and the Puffin being the three species eaten most often. A wide range of other birds includes Herons (taken regularly), Mallard, various waders up to Curlew size, Common and Black Guillemots, Hooded Crows (often the subject of special raids by some owls at communal roosts), and various thrush species. The largest of the seabirds found along these coasts, the Great Black-backed Gull, also falls victim to the Eagle Owl, and further inland the cock Capercaillie, a turkey-sized grouse of coniferous forests, has also been killed.

The Great Horned Owl, like the other eagle owls, can tackle large and formidable prey. This one is wrestling with a large snake.

The Ural Owl feeds on a wide range of small- to medium-sized mammals and birds.

Birds of prey, too, feature in the list, all presumably taken while roosting and including large species like Rough-legged Buzzards, Goshawks, and Peregrines and smaller ones such as Merlins and Sparrowhawks. Another species which Dr Willgohs has studied in great detail, the huge White-tailed Eagle, seems immune to attack from Eagle Owls but apparently its young are not and it seems that even quite large eaglets have occasionally been taken from eyries along the coast. Owls, too, are by no means safe from the attentions of their large cousins: several species are taken quite regularly and even the almost equally large Snowy Owl has figured in prey remains. So has another adult Eagle Owl!

Over many years, the Finnish owl expert,

Heimo Mikkola, has gathered together an enormous quantity of information on owls and other birds of prey killing and eating one another in Europe, and there is no doubt about which species features most prominently in his lists – the Eagle Owl. This redoubtable bird has been recorded as a predator of nearly all Europe's diurnal raptors except the very largest eagles and the vultures. It clearly kills appreciable numbers of Buzzards and Kestrels, as well as a good many Peregrines, Goshawks, and Rough-legged Buzzards. It is also known to have taken all the other European owls except the Great Grey (and there seems no reason to believe that these may not fall victim occasionally), most commonly killing Long-eared and Tawny Owls

but also a good number of Tengmalm's, Hawk, and Little Owls. The Eagle Owl is most certainly a formidable killer and the situation is made worse for its fellow predators by the fact that it is often highly intolerant of other birds of prey within its own territorial bounds. Indeed, Dr Mikkola asserts that up to 5 per cent of its total prey may consist of other birds of prey and that these may make up as much as 36 per cent of all the bird food consumed in some regions.

No other European owl can match the Eagle Owl in this respect, although the Snowy Owl is known to have killed owls and raptors at least up to the size of Rough-legged Buzzards and some medium-sized owls may prey regularly on some of their smaller cousins. The Great Grey Owl is a notable exception – for all its size, it is very tolerant of its neighbours even when these are other owls or hawks, and there are only a few records of it ever killing them.

It seems that the Eagle Owl itself is virtually immune from attack by other bird predators or, at least, is only very rarely killed; certainly no

other owl is likely to worry it at night. Medium-sized and small European owls are also taken in fair numbers by some of the day-hunting birds of prey, especially by the big and powerful Goshawk. Presumably the victims, either owls or hawks, do not always succumb without a struggle: there is in the literature an account of a Common Buzzard taking a Tawny Owl at a roost site during the times when myxomatosis was rife and a general scarcity of Rabbits forced Buzzards to turn to alternative prey. The owl was eventually killed, but not before it had put up a considerable fight – the Buzzard had particular difficulty in freeing itself from the powerful grip of the owl's talons on its own legs.

On the arctic tundra which is its natural habitat, the Snowy Owl preys mainly on lemmings and arctic species of hares, with an assortment of other small mammals and various medium-sized birds and their young making up the balance of its diet. When a pair began to breed in Shetland in 1967, it was of considerable interest to see what prey species they would

Above left
The versatile and powerful Eagle Owl is not only a killer of many mammals and birds but a predator on other owls and many birds of prey.

Above
Learning how to deal with a mouse, a young Tengmalm's Owl.

93

turn to in the absence of both lemmings and hares. In the event, they turned readily to a numerous medium–sized mammal, the Rabbit, and to two birds that are both common on the island of Fetlar, Oystercatchers and Arctic Skuas. The birds were mostly taken during the short hours of darkness, presumably mainly from their roost sites but probably sometimes from their nests, too. A variety of other birds, including a number of waders and their young, plus mice on occasions, supplemented the food supply.

This brief survey of some of the prey preferences of a few species in Europe shows how owls apportion the prey available to them according to their habitats and their hunting abilities. While we have concentrated on European examples, similar studies showing broadly similar patterns have been carried out in the New World and it is to be hoped that in the not too distant future we shall begin to find out more about some of the little-known owls of other regions. But we must now turn to another aspect of the feeding ecology of owls, namely how their numbers and distribution can be affected by the availability of their food supply. In introducing this topic we can do no better than to look at another of the classic studies of bird predators carried out by the Craighead brothers in the United States on the populations of hawks and owls in a small area in Michigan.

Their main study area covered 14·5 hectares (36 acres) of basically agricultural land with a good scattering of small woods and copses, where Great Horned and Screech Owls were the resident species and Long-eared and Short-eared Owls were present in winter. As we might expect, the Great Horned Owl was an adaptable and versatile predator, but even so its fortunes were to some extent linked to the abundance of two species of mice, as were those of the other owls and the diurnal birds of prey.

These mice were very numerous during the first winter of the study, 1941-42, but their estimated winter population six years later was less than one-third of the earlier total. While the resident Great Horned Owls were sufficiently non-specialist to take this in their stride and to maintain a similar population in both winters, there was a marked reduction in the numbers of the two wintering owls which relied much more on the mice. There were seven Long-eareds in 1941–42, but none at all in 1947–48, while the corresponding totals for Short-eareds were up to thirty-one and only four. Similarly, several species of diurnal raptors known to feed mainly on the mice were twice as numerous in the earlier winter. These figures showed quite clearly that the densities of wintering owls and hawks were closely geared to the numbers of their prey.

A number of other studies, in both the New and the Old Worlds, have shown that the nomadic and partially migratory Short-eared Owl tends to concentrate its numbers in areas where its preferred small rodent prey is most numerous,

breeding at high densities in vole years and producing large families – with many young surviving if the food supply lasts – and similarly occurring in strength in winter whenever voles or similar small mammals are particularly numerous. While this species wanders in winter according to the availability of its prey, only Short-eared Owls from the more northerly populations are true migrants in the normal sense. Insectivorous birds, for example, are true migrants in that they may breed in temperate regions in summer and then undertake regular migrations to warmer quarters in search of a new food supply. A few owls fall into the category of true migrants, the Eurasian Scops Owl being a notable example.

At the opposite end of the scale to the migratory and nomadic owls we find a wholly sedentary species like the Tawny Owl which remains faithful to its own 'patch' season after season. There will be times when prey is much harder to come by than others and the Tawny Owl's breeding production may change accordingly when this happens at nesting time, but no matter what the season this owl remains where it is rather than moving out in search of a better living, depending on its experience and its intimate knowledge of its home territory to get the most out of a reduced small mammal population and also relying on its versatility as a predator to improve its chances of survival.

Somewhere between these extremes lies the Barn Owl, normally regarded as a sedentary bird and no doubt deserving the title in most circumstances. It has been found, however, that after years when prey has been abundant and the owls have reared many young a decline in prey numbers will induce European Barn Owls not only to breed less productively – or even not at all – but also to wander far afield in winter. Here then is yet another example of how the balance between predator and prey is maintained, with the controlling factor being the abundance or otherwise of the prey and not the numbers of the predators themselves. Lots of prey means more predators, either in summer or winter, and a high rate of breeding, but when the prey population declines the predators are left with two alternatives, either or both of which may apply: starvation or emigration. A fresh start will then be made by the survivors, now present at a lower density than formerly and often rearing many fewer young, and the whole cycle begins again.

There are many complexities in the predator-prey cycle wherever the environment itself is a complex one with many adjoining habitats and sources of food and the general rules we have outlined above can be best observed in action where there are relatively more straightforward ecosystems: this is the case in the great forest zone or taiga of the north and on the tundra itself. The owls living there show much more marked population fluctuations than their cousins living at lower latitudes.

In the boreal forests, coniferous trees predominate, mainly various kinds of spruce, pine, and larch, with a varying admixture of broad-leaved species like birches and aspens. All the cone-bearing trees have a cyclic rhythm of their own, and ultimately these rhythms govern the life cycles of the many animals which rely, directly or indirectly, on the trees' productivity for their own survival. Maximum cone production occurs about every third or fourth year and birds and squirrels feeding on the seeds within the cones will reach their greatest numbers in these bumper years. But in the year following its maximum fruiting, a tree will go through a 'resting period' and hardly produce any new cones at all – then large numbers of birds like crossbills, which depend almost entirely on the cones and their seeds, must move off in search of new sources of food. In so doing they may produce large-scale irruptions out of their normal range and invasions into new areas which often carry them much further south than is normal. Squirrels, on the other hand, cannot fly away and face a heavy mortality instead through gradual starvation, with only small numbers surviving until the whole process begins again.

The amount of conifer seeds reaching the forest floor produces exactly the same sort of ebb and flow among the ground-dwelling voles, mice, and lemmings which eat them – the excellent feeding provided in good years allowing them to breed so profusely that, in local situations at least, their numbers may even reach plague proportions. As long as these small rodents are enjoying such a food bonanza, the birds and animals which in turn feed upon them also increase and multiply – Great Grey, Tengmalm's (Boreal), and Hawk Owls among them. Then comes the crash, just as we have described it before; the food supply is soon exhausted and the rodent population decimated, quickly followed by the death or dispersal of the predators that, once again, must move away altogether or, if they stay and survive, tighten their belts until the good times come again. Following a serious crash, birds like the Hawk Owl may wander very widely and appear far beyond the limits of their normal distribution.

Obviously, there is great variation in these rhythms of alternating plenty and famine: the cycles are at different stages for different species in different areas at any given point in time so that, in relative terms, the results of lean years may have a more or less local result with predators only moving to another taiga area. There will also be those years, however, when crop failures will occur over very large areas at the same time and it is at such times – especially when they also coincide with a breeding peak among the taiga birds – that the most spectacular irruptions of birds will occur.

Beyond the boreal forests lies the tundra, a vast and desolate-looking landscape without trees, held fast under ice and snow for two-thirds of the year or more, and vegetated with a low-growing carpet of mosses, lichens, small plants, and stunted, prostrate shrubs. It looks a most inhospitable place, but in reality it is very much alive during the short but fruitful arctic summer. No-one who has set foot on the tundra in the summer can fail to be impressed by the abundant and colourful flowers, the swarms of insects, and the wealth of breeding birds occurring there.

The big Snowy Owl is the major bird predator of the tundra and one of its main sources of food is the lemming population. There are several species of lemming, small, fat-looking rodents which live in low vegetation and survive the long, harsh winters in their tunnel systems beneath the snow. Lemmings are prolific breeders and when conditions are right for them their numbers swell enormously, reaching a peak after about four years when their immense numbers simply exhaust the supplies of the vegetation on which they depend. It is then, in the so-called 'lemming years', that the famous mass migrations of these little animals take place when they die in vast numbers. Even in years following lemming movements evidence of their passing can be seen: the author has seen hundreds of dead Norway Lemmings exposed by melting snows in the arctic spring where presumably their bodies had been preserved after being covered in the previous autumn.

As we would expect, their predators fluctuate in numbers along with them in much the same way that we have seen with other species in other habitats. It is worth mentioning, however, that lemming movements can last for more than a single year so that carnivores and birds of prey may well enjoy more than one season feasting on the rich supply of mammal food made available to them. Once again, there will come a time when the lemmings are no more, with the inevitable consequences. Snowy Owls will once more turn elsewhere for new sources of food. The big, white owls are not entirely dependent on lemmings, however, but also take large numbers of other animals like Arctic and Snowshoe Hares. These, too, have cyclic population fluctuations but with them the whole process takes rather longer and peaks are reached at about ten year intervals. It is when the crashes in hare and lemming populations happen to coincide that the most spectacular movements of Snowy Owls take place. There has been a number of notable ones, both in Eurasia and the New World, but so far the biggest have occurred in North America where the area of continuous tundra in the north of the continent is particularly vast. There was an incredibly large dispersal of owls in the winter of 1926–27 when over 2300 were recorded in the United States alone.

We have now sketched an outline showing how owl numbers and reproduction rates are governed by the availability of their prey, but in leading on to these matters from their characteristics and their methods of hunting we have missed out one very important chapter in their lives, that is, how they actually set up home and rear their young. This topic, plus some observations on other aspects of their home lives, are discussed in the next chapter.

The home life of owls

For the greater part of their lives, most owls are rather solitary birds. They are not particularly tolerant of one another, nor do they normally occur even in small groups, let alone flocks. Most of them only come together with others of their kind during the breeding season or, with some species, at communal roosts in winter.

Some birds, of course, find safety in numbers. One bird in a flock has some chance of escaping an attack by a predator, and similarly birds nesting in colonies find that this way of life has survival value – to go further, birds in flocks at breeding grounds can even drive away many types of would-be predators so that all stand a chance of survival. Birds which have the habit of feeding in flocks are often those with an abundant food supply or those which must seek their food in certain restricted areas. There is always enough to go round and hundreds and even thousands of birds can feed happily side by side without competing with one another.

The situation is rather different for predatory birds. They are always much less numerous than the prey species which control their numbers in the last resort and, in effect, are always competing with one another for the available supplies of food. Therefore, if they are to survive, they must be spaced out and must apportion their prey species accordingly. Among the diurnal raptors, only the 'non-active' predators which scavenge or feed on carrion, and some of those that have a mainly insect diet, do not follow this general rule. It is a rule followed virtually without exception among owls. None is truly colonial at breeding time, though the Burrowing Owls of America sometimes nest in loose colonies, and pairs of other species like Short-eared Owls may nest fairly close together and even share hunting grounds when prey is especially abundant. Normally, though, an owl has his or her own territory in which others of the same species are not made welcome and, indeed, in which other sorts of owls and birds of prey may also be 'entering at their own risk'.

In ornithological parlance, a territory is an area in which one bird, or a pair of birds, feeds or nests to the exclusion of others of the same kind: it is advertised and has clearly defined boundaries. The ordinary Robin is a good example of a strictly territorial bird – no other Robin will be tolerated in a bird's own domain and will be challenged, threatened, and, in the last resort, even physically attacked by the owner. The Robin's song, delivered from strategic points within the territory and around its boundary, warns other Robins of the situation, and the red breast is not mere decoration but a signal for recognition and a warning to others. With Robins as well as owls – and many other birds – special behavioural devices are necessary to break down the territorial imperative when the time for pairing and nesting comes around.

Outside the breeding season, owls, which as far as we know do not mate for life in most species, live alone in their preferred habitats. As we have seen, the more nocturnal species hide away, resting and sleeping, by day, often in habitual roost sites, depending for their survival on their unobtrusiveness, their immobility, and their superb camouflage. When the time for them to become active comes around, they patrol the bounds of their territories, frequently calling to advertise their presence and warn off their neighbours, and largely confining their hunting activities to their own ground. In this way, competition for food is reduced and a regular spacing system is achieved between all the owls of one species in any area.

As we have said, some owls do not quite follow these rules, at least during the non-active part of their day – they will still be spaced apart while hunting but may come together to roost communally. For the most part, the species involved are the owls of the more open type of habitat – the Short-eared and Long-eared Owls being good examples. Long-eared Owls are especially well known for their gregariousness at winter roosts: small parties – which could well be made up of a pair and their surviving young from the previous breeding season – are commonly encountered, groups of ten to twenty are by no means unusual, and even as many as fifty together have been recorded. There are often traditional sites in certain places and very often the only Long-eared Owls most birdwatchers ever see are those they encounter at their local roost, if they are lucky enough to have one.

When we see a group of roosting Long-eared Owls and manage to observe them without disturbing them, it is difficult to escape an impression of general friendliness among the birds as they sit, quietly relaxed, and often quite close to one another, in favoured trees and bushes. It has been suggested that these normally rather solitary birds may even exhibit social tendencies at roosts – that is, they like one another's company – and even that they may somehow be able to regulate their own numbers and breeding performance by knowing how many owls are alive and well in their area. There may be some truth in either or both of these theories – although the latter one does seem a little far-fetched – but both are difficult to prove or even evaluate much beyond the guessing stage. What does seem clear is that there is some survival value to the owls in communal roosting and it also seems likely that the availability of really suitable sites may determine how many owls roost in them.

Most owls are active by night, so that the question arises as to how they maintain their territories. They obviously cannot see very much of one another, for all their excellent night vision, and almost all owls lack really distinctive plumage features or striking pattern and colour which serve as either recognition or warning features. Such things are often very prominent in day-living birds with strongly territorial behaviour – and even in some other nocturnal birds, such as the nightjars, many of which have white flashes or patches in conspicuous places on their wings and tails. Visual characteristics are clearly not too important among the nocturnal owls. It is probably enough that an owl's very distinctive general outline and its movements can be seen easily by its fellows, and that further clues to its identity and its mood or intentions can be provided by the ear-tufts which are so much a feature of many owls (nearly half the total number of species). As we have said already, these appendages are often used in recognition and in contact between owls.

Nocturnal owls communicate mainly by voice. Many owls are very vocal indeed, and clearly their well-developed voices compensate for the limitations darkness imposes upon them. Almost all the owls that have been studied in any detail have been found to possess a well-developed 'language', an extensive vocal repertoire which includes calls used to threaten, to mark out territories, to maintain contact with an unseen mate, in courtship, and so on.

One of the main ingredients of an owl's repertoire is its song. It may seem strange to think of owls as singing, compared to the pleasant, musical performances of other birds but, simple though they may often be in form, some owl calls or combinations of calls have the same function as the melodies produced by many garden and woodland birds. Perhaps the best-known owl voice of all is the song of the Tawny Owl, the long, far-carrying, quavering hooting so beloved of film and television producers depicting scenes at night. Other owls sing in different ways: the eagle owls with short, basso hoots; little owls with their short, monotonously repeated, tooting notes; the screech owls with their trills. Other owls soon respond when one of their number begins to sing – on a still night they sing almost in chorus, answering one another across kilometres of countryside, advertising their presence and staking their claims to ownership of a territory. Female owls hear these songs too and, at the appropriate time of year, are attracted towards them. Some have their own special answering calls, recognized by the male and breaking down the first barrier to entry into a territory and eventual pairing. Some female owls go one stage further and sing themselves in reply, so that the two birds actually perform duets – this is known, for example, in some fish owls, in screech owls, eagle owls, Little Owls and Spectacled Owls, to name a few. It is not long before all the owls recognize one another by voice and know where their neighbours' territories are. With this knowledge some form of equilibrium is achieved whereby they will remain good neighbours as long as there is no trespassing!

The relatively simple form of many owl songs renders them fairly easy to mimic, which can be very useful to ornithologists trying to locate owls in the dark, to map their territories, and to find out more about them. Imitating owls can also be useful simply to observe an owl and may, in addition, be helpful in attracting down other birds that instantly mob any owl they see or hear. The author has successfully brought down Tawny Owls by replying to the songs of territorial males, and has also performed a fairly satisfactory duet at quite close quarters with a very perplexed Little Owl!

Those owls which hunt by day are much less vocal than the nocturnal species. They can, after all, rely more on the visual contact used by many other birds, to the extent that they may use visual displays in advertising their territories and attracting mates. The Short-eared Owl, for example, will fly high above its territory with curiously exaggerated wing-beats, the deep, purposeful down-beats of the long wings and the pauses on the upstroke causing the bird's whole body to swing up and down quite markedly, and will also display by clapping their wings together beneath the body. They sing in flight, too, with a deep, rather quiet, but surprisingly far-carrying 'boo-boo-boo' note. On the other hand, Snowy Owls hoot from the ground or perches in open country, again with deep-pitched calls with great carrying power, so that their basic territorial proclamations are often made vocally.

In passing, we may wonder why a largely nocturnal species such as the Barn Owl should have such strikingly white, or in some races at least very pale, plumage? The answer probably lies in that, while they have a very wide and interesting vocal repertoire, Barn Owls have no actual song comparable to that of many other owls. It would seem, therefore, that their distinctive and very visible colouring is an important means of visual communication between individual Barn Owls.

One important function of owl song is the attraction by the male of a mate into his territory but once a female owl arrives, how will she be accepted as a potential partner and not be driven away or otherwise attacked by the male? The answering calls possessed by some owls and also the habit of singing in duet helps, as we have

During courtship, male owls may feed their intended mates. This behaviour continues through the breeding cycle, as with these nesting Snowy Owls.

said, to bring birds together, but more is required of her than these initial responses. Earlier in the book we hinted that the actual behaviour of a bird plays an important part in communication, and this is never more true than at the time of pair formation. The male's instinct is to drive off any other owl venturing into his domain and it should be remembered that as there is no visible distinction between the sexes a male owl probably does not recognize a female on sight. She must adopt a type of submissive behaviour towards the male which will reduce his aggressive first instincts and instead attract him so that he recognizes her for what she is and in his turn changes over to a new pattern of behaviour – his courtship display. Unfortunately, as with so many aspects of owl biology, our knowledge of how all this comes about is unknown for many species and at best only partly known for many more but a few observations for some of the better-studied species will serve to show, in outline at least, how the whole process works.

Very few descriptions of the courtship displays of the Tawny Owl have been published in the otherwise extensive accounts of this species' life and habits, but the author has been lucky enough to watch pairs courting on two occasions and has listened to the vocalizations of other wooing pairs on several more. One of the most striking features of Tawny Owl courtship is

indeed the 'conversation' which apparently goes on between the two birds. Though it is difficult to know which bird is saying what, the impression is that the male does most of the talking. There is a variety of quiet, cooing and clucking notes, little sighs and wails, and numerous other sounds, sometimes interspersed with bill-clicking noises which are commonly made by many owls in their various displays.

In both instances seen by the author, the two owls were on a large, lateral branch of a big tree, perched only about a metre apart. The cock bird sidled along towards the female, swaying slightly from side to side and bowing towards her, and then retreated – a performance he repeated several times. At times his plumage was fluffed out in a relaxed and presumably confident gesture, but at others it was pressed in tight against his body – which would seem to indicate a submissive gesture. Occasionally, physical contact was made with the female when what seemed like mutual bill nibbling movements took place. The ultimate sequence, copulation, was not seen on either occasion. In one case, the birds were disturbed by passers-by and in the other, the female suddenly flew off, closely followed by the male. Nevertheless, there was no mistaking the intimacy being established between the two birds. Indeed, once the pair bond has been formed, Tawny Owls (and no

98

doubt other species, too) always give the impression of being extremely happily married – they sit close together, side by side and often touching one another, and behaviour like the bill nibbling mentioned above is frequent.

Rather similar conversation pieces have been watched and described for Barn Owls, which also perch close together and may both sway and roll with much mutual nibbling and physical contact. The male rolls his head noticeably, tending to look downwards so that his crown is presented to the female rather than his face – a form of display used in other cirumstances too. An injured Barn Owl kept by the author used to display in much the same way when disturbed – a slow, side-to-side, rolling movement in which his big, rounded head became very prominent.

Courtship feeding, in which the male ritually presents the female with a morsel of food or an item of prey, is well known in many birds including some of the diurnal birds of prey. It is also seen in some owls (and no doubt occurs in the courtships of many others) such as the Tawny and the Eurasian Eagle Owls, and also in the Snowy Owl. Recent studies on the courtship behaviour of this last species have been made in arctic Canada by Philip S Taylor and his published account is well worth summarizing here.

Male Snowy Owls use circling display flights over their territories, as well as the vocal advertisement mentioned already, and one of their displays in the presence of a female is also carried out on the wing. This particular activity seems only to happen when a female is visible, but she need not be close at hand and may indeed be sitting up to 800 metres ($\frac{1}{2}$ mile) away from the male's territory at the time.

The male flies around with exaggerated wing-beats, especially on the up stroke when the wings are briefly held aloft in a 'v' shape, and as he does so his wing action produces much the same sort of up-and-down movement of his body as is seen when Short-eared Owls are display flying. He then descends to the ground. Often, he is carrying a lemming in his bill during this display. Once on the ground, he puts down the lemming and then adopts an erect posture, with his wings partly opened, and may walk and turn slowly about a small area, never straying far from where he landed. As this ground display continues, he tends to lean further forward and to lower his head, at the same time slightly fanning his tail. As he walks and turns, the white upper surfaces of his partly opened wings produce a conspicuous flashing effect, visible over a long distance – and presumably quickly seen and interpreted by a distant female. As this continues, the female will fly to the male and land near him, and often behind him, and will gradually move closer. All the while the male has been avoiding facing her directly and instead shows her his sides or even his back. He continues to do this as she comes closer, sometimes bringing a wing round to hide his front still more. It looks to an observer as if he is deliberately trying to shield the lemming from her gaze and there seems to be some relationship between this movement and the habit many birds of

An Elf Owl at its nest – a natural hole in a tree.

Above
A cavity in a broken tree-trunk provides a home for these Boobook Owls.

Above right
Holes in trees, natural or made by other birds, are favoured by the Pygmy Owl.

Right
Screech Owls in a woodpecker's hole in a *Saguaro* cactus – a site often used by the small Elf Owl.

prey have of 'mantling' with their wings over their prey very soon after they have caught it. Neither the flight nor the ground displays normally last more than a couple of minutes, but are more or less performed alternately in succession until they evoke the desired response from the female. Suitably stimulated, she will adopt a

special posture inviting the male to mate with here; this is the climax of the display.

In common with other birds, owls do not cease ritual behaviour of this sort once the immediate objects of pair formation and mating have been achieved. Although the pair bond has been established, it is necessary to continue the

A Tengmalm's or
Boreal Owl emerging
from its nest hole.

mating behaviour so that it is both strengthened and maintained. The basically hostile urges are never far below the surface so that continuing display is necessary to sublimate them. Thus, parts of the initial courtship behaviour will continue to be used during the breeding cycle, copulation included, and new ceremonies will come into use, such as greeting displays at the nest, and so on. And the male still has his territory to defend against potential interlopers.

The next stage in the affairs of owls is the selection of the actual site for the nest and the rearing of the family. Very likely the male's display will have centred around a site he has already selected, or one which has been used before because once a site is known to be a good one owls may come back and use it again and again. Indeed, the occupation of it may not have ceased at all and it may double up as a roost site in winter.

One of the most remarkable things about birds is the ability many of them have to build nests

Large holes or
fissures in trees are
used by the Ural Owl.

which are small masterpieces of engineering and design in various media. Vegetation of almost every conceivable sort is woven into cups, roofed nests, nests with porches and entrance tunnels, nests suspended in trees or adhering to rock faces and walls, and many more. Nests may be built of mud, sometimes brick by brick in the form of small pellets, even using saliva as cement. Some birds can even sew leaves together very expertly to form warm and watertight homes. Owls, however, are not talented in this way. Few build at all, even in the simplest way, and even those which do make some attempt at home building often merely add a few bits and pieces or carry out minor alterations to existing structures. Owl homes fall into three broad categories.

Firstly, many species use a hole of some sort, often a natural hole in rocks or in a tree, or some sort of fissure or crevice. Holes in buildings may do just as well for some owls. The holes made by other birds or animals are also quite popular: woodpeckers, in particular, are helpful to a number of smaller or middle-sized owls. Holes left behind in the big *Saguaro* cactus provide ready made homes for the tiny Elf Owl in American desert country, while Tengmalm's and Hawk Owls in Europe profit from taking over the vacated holes of the big Black Woodpecker.

Other birds' nests make up the second main group – this time more orthodox structures in trees and bushes. The nests of various species of crow are much favoured by the Long-eared Owl which will also use almost anything else similar in size and structure; for example, the first Long-eared Owl's nest the author ever found was in an old Sparrowhawk's nest. Bigger owls need bigger homes, and species such as the Eurasian Eagle Owl, the Great Horned Owl, and the Great Grey Owl use the old nests of Ravens, buzzards of various kinds, Goshawks, and even Golden Eagles, as well as disused squirrel dreys on occasion. In Africa, Barn Owls, too, have been found using old eagles' nests, and those of other quite large birds like the Hammerkop. Some of the tropical eagle owls apparently do some nest building on their own account, but the efforts attributed to some

The Milky Eagle
Owl uses the old nest
of an eagle or
vulture.

other species, like the Great Grey Owl, for example, may refer only to minor alterations and not to actual construction work.

The third category involves sites which are actually on the ground, of which the nests of Short-eared and Snowy Owls are good examples. These are usually mere scrapes or depressions, although some species may sometimes add a little grass as lining material and tunnels may be made through thick grass into suitable, sheltered spots. Other species which are not normally ground nesters may choose a terrestrial site from time to time. The Tawny Owl is among these as, when there are no trees, may be the Long-eared Owl. Tawny Owls will also sometimes nest on the ground inside the hollow base of a dead tree. Holes in the ground may also be used: the Burrowing Owl is well known for choosing this type of site, and the habit has been recorded in several other species including the Tawny Owl yet again. The author has seen Little Owls nesting in Rabbit burrows, with

Above
A Barn Owl flying to its nest site in a turret; buildings and ruins are often used by this species.

Above right
Barn Owls use all kinds of holes to gain access to build-ings.

Right
In common with other owls, Barn Owls build no nest at all. Here, the young have been reared on an almost bare ledge.

Above left
A Great Grey Owl
using an old Osprey's
nest in Sweden.

Above
Young Long-eared
Owls in an old
crow's nest.

Rabbits as close neighbours. In the prairie and semidesert country where it lives, the Burrowing Owl can use a wide variety of holes made by ground-dwelling mammals: those of the Prairie Dog (a small marmot) are particularly popular, and again owls and mammals will live side by side in apparent harmony. Holes made by armadillos, foxes, and skunks do just as well. All these creatures, the owls included, find these underground homes very useful in sheltering them from the often intense heat of the sun in these open habitats.

We have also mentioned some species which will nest quite readily in buildings. The Barn Owl is the best known of these, but others include essentially woodland species such as the Tawny and Ural Owls, as well as the Little Owl. While this book was being written, the author heard from a friend living in Florida that a pair of Barred Owls had even taken up residence on a balcony in an apartment block!

Equally, a number of owls, and not only those which usually nest in holes, will use specially prepared homes provided by man. Small garden birds are not the only ones that will use nestboxes. Large boxes of traditional design may work quite well, but these are often modified in the light of experience and knowledge of the requirements of a particular species, resulting in several current designs for owl

boxes. Such sophistication is not always necessary, though – many owls breed successfully and apparently in great comfort in such things as old crates and beer barrels. In areas where the old-fashioned barn loft is a thing of the past, or the clearance of old hedgerow trees has removed natural hole sites, Barn Owls have been successfully tempted into even the most modern open barns by the provision of suitable nesting trays positioned close to their roofs. Buildings which have no history of Barn Owl occupation may also help if a suitable access hole is made at one end.

From what we know of their domestic lives, most owls seem to be extremely good and attentive parents and certainly some species have outstanding reputations for the lengths they will go to in the defence of their young. Many owls will launch vigorous physical assaults on bird and animal predators, often delivered with such ferocity and persistence that the would-be raider is soon driven off. Some species are quite unafraid of man and will attack him just as readily as any other potential enemy. For all its even-temperedness towards its owl and hawk neighbours, the Great Grey Owl can be a formidable bird if its home is directly threatened and will strike and buffet human intruders fearlessly – which can be quite an unnerving experience. Even the little American screech

A Burrowing Owl at a typical nest site.

Some owls defend their nests and young vigorously. Here, a Screech Owl strikes at an ornithologist looking at one of her young.

owls will attack people, just as the Barking Owl will in Australia. Without doubt, however, the owls with the most notorious record for their determined assaults on man are the Tawny Owl and the two rather larger and rather similar *Strix* owls, the Ural and the Barred, of Eurasia and America respectively. Between them, these species have seriously injured scores of people – many ornithologists among them – through slashing at their faces with their razor-sharp talons. A number of people have lost eyes as the result of attacks by Tawny and Ural Owls. The clear lesson, if you are thinking of looking at these owls when they are nesting, is to wear suitable protective headgear and, above all, to be very careful: even a sudden thump on the head from a Tawny can be very alarming.

There are plenty of cases on record of Tawny

A Short-eared Owl brooding small young in a typical ground nest site.

Even the Tawny Owl, normally a hole nester, will use other birds' nests occasionally.

gate post to gate post and from fences to small garden trees – never more than a few metres away.

While some owls attack with gusto, others will do nothing at all except make themselves as scarce as possible. Still others, usually those which nest in more open situations, use quite different tactics, based on bluff and deception rather than naked aggression.

Threatening behaviour, rather than actual violence, is often the main defensive tactic used by many birds, some owls included. The main aim will be to terrify the enemy – or to lure him away after an apparently easy target. When danger threatens, an owl will attempt to make itself appear as big and as ferocious as possible, and to do this it will crouch with its wings fanned outwards and all its body feathers fluffed out so that it really does seem to be twice as big as it was before. The great staring eyes add to the illusion (and, with their often vividly coloured irises, may even have a definite threatening function) and very often the whole display is accompanied by bill snapping and angry calls. Displays of this sort are by no means confined to adult owls. Owlets in or near the nest will employ exactly the same tactics and no doubt even manage to deter a number of predators all by themselves.

It is perhaps surprising that the huge Eagle Owl does not attack physically but uses a threat display instead. With such a big, awesome-looking bird, however, the effect can be very

Above
A Tawny Owl nesting on the ground.

Right
Young Burrowing Owls outside a typical nest site.

Owls nesting close to public thoroughfares terrorizing passers-by – so much so that direct action to remove the owls has sometimes been taken. In other cases, even covered walkways have been provided instead! Such energetic defence usually only occurs close to the nest, but clearly there are exceptions. Late one evening, on his way home, the author was literally escorted from a Tawny Owl's territory by a male bird which followed him very closely, flying from

impressive indeed. Some years ago a captive pair which reared young in Edinburgh Zoo reacted very vigorously whenever anybody stayed too long at that part of their aviary where the young were sitting – small, noisy children provoking the biggest and best displays. The effect on the zoo visitors could be quite remarkable! Next door there lived a Rüppell's Griffon, a very large African vulture, which was normally ignored by the owls and which in its turn

ignored them. But on the occasions when the vulture chanced to wander too close to the young he too was instantly subjected to the complete treatment.

The other main form of bluffing behaviour is 'distraction display' where the object of the bird's actions is not so much to overawe the enemy as to lure it away. This behaviour is very well known among many wildfowl and wading birds which use it as their primary means of defence if their families are threatened. An owl will drop one wing, or both, and stumble and shuffle away over the ground, hoping to convince the predator that it is injured or vulnerable. This method works well with many would-be owl catchers that never seem to learn by experience that they are the object of a colossal deception. They often follow eagerly, while the owl takes care to stay just beyond their reach, and once the chase has gone on for long enough for the threat to the vulnerable youngsters to have disappeared, the owl simply gets up and flies back to them.

The reactions of the Shetland Snowy Owls to various intruders have been particularly well documented and are worth mentioning here. Indeed, these owls are probably the most closely and continuously watched members of their tribe anywhere in the world due to the non-stop watch over them maintained by wardens from the Royal Society for the Protection of Birds on the Fetlar Reserve.

Because they are rather large and, to other birds at least, rather obvious, the adult owls – the all-white male especially – are subjected to considerable harassment and mobbing by other birds present on the breeding area or passing through it. Many of these are simply ignored in the time-honoured fashion of all owls, but occasionally there will be retaliation. The male owl has been seen to leap after gulls, terns, and skuas in a most menacing way on a number of occasions. Sheep, ponies, and sheepdogs will be treated to various versions of threat display or distraction tactics and have sometimes been assaulted – though there was also an occasion when a sheep confronted by an irate owl simply walked up to it and outstared it! The owls have no real natural enemies, but sometimes large birds like Great Black-backed Gulls and Great Skuas, which could present a real threat to small owlets, are attacked and driven off. The only birds that persistently outwit the owls are the local Hooded Crows, crafty and resourceful scavengers that seem mainly interested in the owls to rob them. A gang of these grey-vested bandits will usually have some success in their raids, no matter how much and how energetically the cock owl chases them around.

The reserve wardens' duties include regular but very brief inspection visits to the nest itself, to check on the progress of the young, and these always provoke a good deal of display from the adult birds. There is a number of variations on a general theme, but perhaps the following extracts from the author's notebook will give a good impression of what happens. On the occasion in question, a quick look at the nest was necessary to check on the welfare of the youngest chick, which had been having difficulties since it had hatched (how and why this situation arises is discussed later in the chapter). As the approach

A female Snowy Owl feeding a chick on the nest. The white face soon becomes discoloured from dealing with prey brought in by the male.

Right
Tawny Owls readily
take to nestboxes.

Far right
Another Tawny Owl
nestbox – crude yet
effective.

A Great Horned Owl
feeding its young.
Owls are careful
and attentive
parents.

Protective headgear is useful at some owl nests. Here, an angry Great Horned Owl attacks an intruding ornithologist.

Not all owls attack intruders; by making itself as large and fearsome looking as possible, the Long-eared Owl tries to frighten away its enemies.

Young owls, too, like this young Great Horned Owl, can produce quite effective threat displays.

was made to the nest, the female owl came off at once and landed some distance away, barking gruffly; then 'when we arrived at the nest she began an awesome charge towards us, half flying and half running, her feathers fluffed out and almost doubling her size'. This time, she stopped short, merely watching and barking instead of continuing this part-threat, part-distraction display. However, 'the male was much more demonstrative. As we got to the nest, he landed a few yards away – an incredibly fine bird in his anger, pure white but for a few dark spots, with wonderful white-feathered legs and feet and great golden-rimmed eyes. His energetic display consisted of bowing forwards with half-open wings, his plumage ruffled rather like his mate's had been; he barked loudly and then began to tear out tiny pieces of grass from around his feet with his bill. Finally, he began to bow forwards rhythmically, hooting in a very deep, gruff voice.'

Most of this, like similar displays seen by the wardens over the years, was pure show, but there have been occasions when the male has actively attacked observers from the air, hitting them now and then. The angry grass pulling described

above is an example not of pure rage but of what is called 'displacement activity'. Very often, when a bird is subjected to some sort of stress or is confronted by a situation which takes it by surprise, it will behave in a number of curious ways, almost irrationally, doing things (such as going through the motions of feeding or preening) which have no relevance at all to the situation.

We have already seen how owls can be very intolerant of one another as neighbours and how, when they occur together, they may even prey on one another. How is it, then, that different species can in fact exist side by side in the same area and still survive? The answer lies in their not competing with one another too directly, as can be seen if we look at a group of Finnish owls of the genus *Strix* which have been the subjects of detailed studies by Dr Heimo Mikkola.

Here, Great Grey, Ural, and Tawny Owls can occur in the same area. The Great Grey, although the largest of the three, is the most tolerant; it does not trouble the other species and, on account of its great size, is left well alone by them. Also, it feeds primarily on small mammals, especially voles, and is the most

diurnal of the three. The Tawny Owl is the most nocturnal and though it certainly likes voles it takes other small mammals, too, and has a large bird component in its diet; thus, it does not compete with the Great Grey for prey, nor are the two likely to be actually hunting the same area at the same time for more than a small part of any twenty-four-hour period. The Ural Owl takes rather larger mammals and game birds, as well as small mammals; it is not a vole specialist. It also falls somewhere between the other two in being partly nocturnal but also hunting partly by day. Here again, there is no direct competition with the other two for food, and only a partial overlap of hunting times. Where this overlap with the Tawny Owl becomes significant, as sometimes happens, there is a simple if rather brutal solution; it will kill its smaller cousin.

Long-eared and Short-eared Owls may nest very close to one another, but without competing for nest sites. The Short-eared nests on the ground and the Long-eared almost always in a tree. They may well hunt the same prey in exactly the same area, however, but in their case there is a straightforward division of effort: the

Short-eared Owl is largely a daylight hunter, while the night-shift is almost exclusively the province of the very nocturnal Long-eared.

To return to the actual breeding, an important question is the timing of the owls' nesting period. Among many of the temperate zone owls, breeding often begins very early in the year, even when it is technically still winter and snow is on the ground. It may seem an odd time to begin to rear a family, especially because few other birds nest at this time, but there is a purpose to it and early nesting obviously has its advantages to owls or they would not even contemplate it. Once again, we find that the timing of nesting is closely geared to the availability of prey. When the young owls hatch and the whole family's food requirement becomes very much greater, it is spring or early summer and the maximum amount of food is there for the taking. Prey supplies remain good throughout the summer as the owlets grow up and leave the nest and through the often prolonged period (some months in big species like the eagle owls) when they remain dependent on their parents for food, and are also learning to hunt and to fend for themselves. In tropical regions, the breeding

A Great Grey Owl and young. This owl will attack human intruders with great determination.

A Long-eared Owl settling on its eggs. Incubation is carried out by female owls.

period is again allied to prey availability, and is often geared to the wet and dry seasons which form the main weather divisions in many regions. For example, insectivorous Scops Owls nest in spring in southern Europe and have young in the nest in the warm period when insect populations are at their highest. The same species further south in Africa will not breed until what we call the autumn because of the timing of the rains which bring about the greatest abundance of food.

There is some variation among owls as to which sex carries out the various functions. With many, it is the male that chooses the nest site, as part of his display when he attracts and secures his mate, but once mating has occurred and the eggs are laid the nest becomes very much the domain of the hen bird. She alone incubates, while the male hunts for them both and brings prey to her at regular intervals. He also has the main responsibility for guarding the nest site and, of course, still has the maintenance of his territory to look to. Once the young owls hatch and are strong enough to be left on their own, the female may well take her share in hunting for the family, but in some species, such as the Great Grey Owl, the male will continue to be

the provider. Once the young are on the wing, however, both parents share in seeking food for them.

At this point, it is worth mentioning that monogamy is the rule among owls. For an active, predatory bird, polygamy is not a particularly attractive prospect unless prey is either superabundant or very easily obtained. Therefore, very few males will take on more than one mate. This does happen to some extent among the harriers, but the pressures on one male bird with two (or even more) families to feed can obviously be considerable, more so if he has to work hard to catch prey, and the end result is often a reduced fledging rate among the young in all the nests under his charge. There is an exception to every rule and bigamy has been recorded among Snowy Owls, but it is rare even with this species and its effects are little known. It was, therefore, of considerable interest when the Shetland Snowy Owls – already rather unusual members of their species – looked like following the example of some of their arctic relatives. In recent seasons, a second female has competed, with some initial success, for the attentions of the solitary adult male; fortunately for him, if perhaps unfortunately

A Barn Owl's nest with eggs, newly hatched young, and prey remains.

Ten eggs in a Short-eared Owl's nest – indicative of an abundance of prey and a year when the production of young may be high.

for our scientific curiosity, nothing has ever come of these potential double marriages. It would probably be a good thing for the young owls if the situation remains that way because in several recent years the owls have had considerable trouble in rearing young from even one nest.

Owl's eggs are white. This follows the pattern common among other hole nesters which presumably have little need of any camouflage for their eggs or for any other distinctive markings. On the other hand, it is also of interest to find that owls which do not nest in holes – and this means many of them – have white eggs, too. In their case, some reliance must be placed on the excellent camouflage of the sitting female

providing protection for what would certainly be very conspicuous objects. It has been said that white eggs are useful to birds nesting in dark holes and crannies – they can be seen easily – and it would seem likely that there is some truth in the suggestion.

Most owls' eggs are more markedly spherical than those of other birds, but there are exceptions: both the Barn Owl and the Great Grey Owl lay rather more conventionally shaped eggs. It is difficult to be sure why owls' eggs should be shaped as they are. Certainly the most extreme egg shapes in terms of pointedness are found among those birds which nest in the most precarious places – Guillemots on narrow sea-cliff ledges, for example – where the more

A male Long-eared Owl bringing prey to the female – he does the hunting while she tends the nest.

elongated the egg the less likely it is to roll off into space if accidentally pushed about. Orthodox eggs fit very neatly together into small nests and can be covered efficiently by a sitting bird but they also occur in open nest sites and others very similar to those used by owls, and why should owls not have eggs which fit neatly under them? Presumably owls' eggs are, in fact, the right shape for owls to brood them without difficulty so that we are left with a number of unanswered questions.

The number of eggs in a clutch can vary considerably. We have already seen that the number of young reared in any one season will depend on the amount of prey available and that more young will be reared in good prey years than in bad ones. Clutch size, then, is an integral part of the automatic family planning system we see operating so perfectly in a number of owl species. Thus, between three and seven eggs are normal for Barn Owls, but in good years as many as eleven have been recorded. Short-eared Owls have laid as many as twelve, and Snowy Owls up to thirteen – in both species numbers similar to the norm quoted for Barn Owls are more usual. In those seasons when things are going really badly, no eggs may be laid at all.

Another very general rule is that birds breeding in the tropics tend to produce smaller clutches than those in higher latitudes. This can be seen on a more restricted scale even in Europe,

117

A Ural Owl incubating. This species often uses the old nest site of a buzzard or Goshawk.

or in the British Isles where the average clutch size of a bird like the Song Thrush is greater in the far north of Scotland than it is in the southernmost counties of England. The same general principle applies among owls, even within the same species. Those birds which nest further north stand rather more chance of being endangered by adverse weather conditions or food shortages than their cousins far to the south, that have a usually more settled environment, and have to put much more effort into a single breeding season to produce a comparable number of surviving young.

Owls do not lay their eggs all at once – one to four days may elapse between layings – but unlike many birds they do not generally await the completion of their clutch before beginning

to incubate. Some species, such as the Pygmy Owl, do wait but most owls studied so far begin to incubate as soon as the first egg is laid. This means that it will hatch some time before the second egg, which in its turn will hatch before the third, and so on, so that the resulting brood of owlets will consist of birds of a variety of ages and sizes. This process is known as asynchronous hatching. Once again, we see the family planning system common to owls and many birds of prey coming into play.

Although it often seems alien to us (and is a rule man has long disputed and ceased to observe), nature has an inexorable law that only the fittest will survive. Translated into owl nest terms, this means that the first comers among the chicks will be the strongest and the most

Many owls nest
early in the year.
Snow was falling
when this Great
Horned Owl was
photographed on her
eggs.

A Barn Owl's eggs.
Owl's eggs are white
and rounded in
shape.

vigorous, getting the most food and being able
to dominate their younger brothers and sisters.
The smallest young must be content with food
remains and often cannot eat at all until their
superiors are replete. Only when food is plentiful do they stand much chance of surviving. If
the youngest chick or chicks die of starvation,
they may well be eaten by their bigger brothers
and sisters, or may even be fed to them by the
parent birds. It seems very harsh by our standards, but the end result of all this is that only the
fittest owls survive to carry on the line. There is

no place in the hard world these young owls will
shortly enter for any weaklings or any bird that
cannot look after itself.

In their early days of life, the baby owls wear a
coat of short, white down which, when they are
between one and two weeks old, will be replaced by a second down, which may this time
be grey or brownish, of rather longer feathers.
This forms their protection against the elements
once they begin to grow up and are no longer so
closely brooded by the female. In due course, the
true feathers begin to grow through this down

A remarkable photograph at a Tawny Owl's nest where the back has been removed: the adult enters with a mouse for the owlet.

and, because many young owls will actually vacate their nests long before they can fly, owlets are often seen in 'half-and-half' plumage, with both down and feathers present. Even fully feathered young owls will still show some signs of down, especially around their heads, shoulders, and underparts.

While the young are small and the female remains in close attendance at the nest, the male brings in all the prey to the family and, at first, that presented to the young consists of rather small items. Equally, the adult owl will

Young Ural Owls
at a typical nest site.

decapitate small mammals and birds, or crush their skulls with its bill, before giving them to the young. Larger prey items will be dismembered and the young given selected parts of them. Sometimes, as happens, for example, with the Snowy Owl, the male bird may even establish larders or 'food depots' where prey items are stored temporarily. But the young grow fast and it is not long before the biggest and most voracious among them can be given complete animals and birds to swallow whole. Soon after this stage has been reached the adults

Many owls lay their eggs at intervals but incubate from the laying of the first one. This results in a staggered hatch and a family of youngsters of different ages and sizes.

can simply leave prey in or near the nest for the young to pick up and deal with by themselves.

Long before they are able to fly, the young of some species will leave the nest itself and wander into the branches of trees, or surrounding vegetation if they come from a ground nest. There they continue to be attended by their parents as they continue to grow up and begin to learn something about their surroundings. Obviously they are very vulnerable at this stage in their young lives and the very act of dispersal means that any prowling predator will not come upon them as a group and kill them all. Thus, dispersal has a definite survival value, even among those species in which parents defend them most vigorously. Young owls often have characteristic, loud begging cries, uttered even in daylight by some nocturnal species, which must some-

times lead to their undoing. This noisiness often helps the naturalist who may not have found the owl's nest in the first place. Very often the first indication of Long-eared Owls breeding in an area comes when the young are heard.

During all this time, the young owls are exercising themselves, gradually growing stronger and bolder and carrying out vigorous wing movements. They may wander some way from their starting point in this way, but one day there comes the time when they will make their first real flights – often clumsy attempts which can be very humorous to watch.

It is probably as well to insert a general word of warning at this point. Young and partly helpless owls which cannot yet fly but are out of the nest are frequently found and picked up by well-meaning people who assume the young are

A young Eagle Owl
in its protective
coat of woolly down.

A young Tawny Owl
still in down but
with the wing and
tail feathers just
starting to develop.

Many owls require more study. Here, an ornithologist is delousing a Little Owl to find which parasites live on its body.

Expert care for a young Snowy Owl in Shetland. This bird tore its wing on a barbed wire fence but fortunately was rescued.

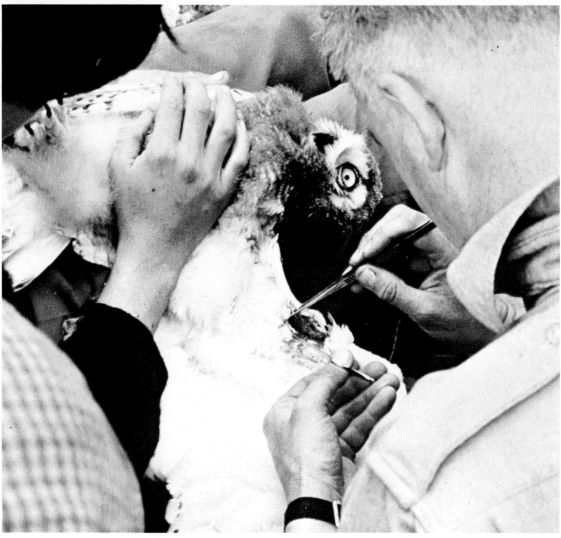

The Little Owl is
beneficial to man
because of the
numbers of insects
it eats.

Above
Exercise is important for the fast-growing owlet. Here, a three-week-old Long-eared Owl tries out its stubby wings.

lost orphans or have fallen out of their nest. This can occasionally be the case but most owlets picked up are probably coping quite well and almost certainly their parents will know where they are. They are usually best left alone or, if they are in a position of obvious risk, such as sitting in the middle of a busy road, they can be moved into a hedgerow or similar safe place and left to their own devices. Once taken home and treated with lavish care, a young owl very quickly becomes incredibly tame. It will often be very difficult to introduce the bird back into the wild or quite impossible if the bird has lost all fear of humans. Owls live a long time and make delightful pets but they belong in the wild and, in Britain, it is against the law to take young owls to keep as pets. Injured owls are another matter – they can be taken into care quite legally, as long as the intention is to release them when they are fit again, although they may be kept if there is no hope of their ever living a natural life again.

Some time elapses – several months with the biggest species – before young owls become fully independent. They are provided with prey by their parents as they slowly begin to acquire the skills necessary to the owl way of life and, most important, learn by trial and error and constant practice to hunt and kill for themselves. The instinct to hunt and kill seems to be inborn, but the skill to do it properly has to be acquired. At last, the time comes when a young owl has to make its own way in the world. Some may maintain a loose contact with their parents, for example, those species with communal roosting habits, but most must move away from the area where they grew up and find their own roost sites and territories for the winter. For some owls this involves travelling some distance or even migrating – either rather locally or, as true migrants, to distant parts.

However well they have passed through these dangerous first months of life and however proficient they have become as hunters, owls in the first winter of their lives are at their most vulnerable. Those which reach full independence still have many trials ahead of them so that it comes as no surprise to learn that it is during the first year of their life that mortality among them is most heavy. We know this from bird ringing. This involves the capture of the young (or adults) by ornithologists who then place a lightweight metal alloy ring, or band, around one leg. This causes the bird no discomfort and is soon ignored by the wearer. Each ring carries a unique number and the name and address, in

126

Two recently fledged
Eurasian Scops Owls
strike a picturesque
pose on the bones of
a domestic animal.

Far left
Young owls leave the nest before they are fully feathered. This young Screech Owl flies well but still has much down remaining in its plumage.

An immature Snowy Owl showing the heavily barred plumage typical of a young bird.

abbreviated form, of the ringing authority. If the young owl is ever recaptured alive, or, more likely, found dead, reference back to the original ringing details can tell us a certain amount about the bird's age and its place of origin. Once these ringing returns are numerous enough for any one species, we can begin to build up a good picture of how long they live and how far they wander.

A great many young Tawny Owls are ringed each year in Europe – notwithstanding the hazards of handling them when their parents are around, as they often are – and from these we know that their life expectancy in the first year is very short. In Switzerland, for example, ringing returns show that nearly half the independent young perish before they are a year old; in Sweden the figure is even higher at 67 per cent. There is some fall in these figures during the second year, and a still further drop in the third; by the time it reaches this sort of age an owl has become something of a veteran and the longer it lives the better its chances of surviving longer become.

So far, then, we have looked at some of the matters which influence an owl's way of life, and have seen how superbly adapted the bird is to cope with its environment. In theory, this is all very well – but we must now move on to look at one very important factor which can drastically alter the tidy, natural sequences we have described: this factor is our own direct and indirect involvement with owls.

Owls and man

In this final chapter, we must look at how owls and man get along together, posing the question 'Can we – or should we – coexist with owls, and are we doing so?' This is important because man's influence over those other animals with which he shares the Earth has never been as widely felt as it is today. Man has found ways of circumventing many of the natural laws which govern the so-called 'balance of nature' and there is no doubt that some of his activities are detrimental to certain forms of wildlife. There are those who hold the view that all this is the inevitable result of man's own evolution – in other words, that anything which cannot withstand the pressures his civilization puts on the environment deserves its fate. In effect they are using the old 'survival of the fittest' cliché, the fittest in their view being man. Others would hold an opposite view – that because man has evolved a sense of responsibility and an ability to choose, to some extent at any rate, the sort of world in which he wishes to live, he has a responsibility to see that his own progress is not needlessly wasteful in terms of destroying wildlife and its habitats. The second point of view, which is shared by probably all naturalists, suggests that man can go on increasing his hold over the world in all sorts of ways but that there is no need for him to do so at the expense of wildlife. Wildlife and man can co-exist in harmony, even if to some degree it is on man's terms.

Following the second line of reasoning – which more or less expresses the view of conservationists – we must try to see how owls fit into the scheme of things as far as man is concerned. As a start, it will be helpful if we look at the background of man's relationships with these birds and see how he feels about them.

Most people see the occasional wild owl, or if not will see owls in captivity at zoos, bird gardens, and wildlife parks; at any rate, everyone knows what an owl looks like. Man has indeed been familiar with owls for a very long time. We know that prehistoric man was aware of owls – they have been represented in his cave paintings, for example. Perhaps the best known owls in prehistoric art are the Snowy Owls depicted at Trois Frères, in France. It is reasonable to suppose that this species was an inhabitant of many areas, where it no longer breeds, after the last Ice Age when the habitats we now associate with the far north were present over large areas of Europe. Other remains which have been found from this period in man's

history show that the Snowy Owl was eaten by man – its young are still eaten by Eskimos in some regions. Other species have figured in prehistoric remains, such as the Barn Owl, which was probably also taken for food. In more recent times, fortunately, owls have not been regarded as a source of food although the Collared Scops Owl provides an interesting exception. Owl soup formed a recipe of the Chinese until quite recently, not merely as a recommended dish but as one with important medicinal properties: it was thought to be helpful in curing consumption and rheumatism. The unfortunate Collared Scops Owl was the chief ingredient.

For many thousands of years, owls and men probably co-existed with very little friction – if any at all. A few owls may have been taken for culinary purposes in some areas, but basically man did not see them in any sense as a competitor and it seems highly unlikely that they were ever harmful to his interests. Nevertheless, man did not ignore owls. As he encountered these strange, silent, nocturnal fliers, or listened to their often weird calls, he built up a whole range of superstitions about them – a curious mixture of feelings in which the owl figured as a good or bad creature. In fact, this ambivalence almost led down the centuries to a 'love-hate' relationship, many of the facets of which we can still recognize today.

If we consider the 'love' side of the relationship first (bearing in mind that 'love' is in reality too strong a word for what man felt – some affection perhaps, but no more), the first thing we encounter is an actual identification between man and owls. This is based simply on the appearance of the birds: they are upright, a posture we associate with humans, they have forward-facing eyes set in rounded faces on a wide head and even some of the sounds they make are rather human.

This vaguely human look which owls undeniably have has no doubt been a contributory factor in man's assessment of them as wise birds. Perhaps any creature which resembles us, however slightly, seems automatically more intelligent than other forms. Another factor which has given rise to this attribute of wisdom arises from one of the natural defence mechanisms we have looked at elsewhere in the book. This is their habit of sitting very still, especially when being watched and when they are using their camouflage in an attempt to remain unseen. We associate this very immobility, seeing and hearing all but uttering little, with a wise outlook on life. 'Wise old owls' appear in many animal stories, sometimes in the garb of schoolmasters, often dispensing wisdom to the other animals (with which, of course, they never have any predatory relationships). There is no doubt that an owl is a cartoonist's ideal as a creature for caricature and, even though owls are no more wise than most other birds – and a good deal less 'clever' than others – it is fortunate that in western art and literature we find them as wise and amiable characters because this creates an attitude of mind towards owls which probably stays with us ever afterwards.

On the more superstitious side, owls have been regarded as useful to us in many other ways, too: various parts of their anatomies have been seen in various cultures as having useful medicinal properties and these have included, not surprisingly, the birds' eyes, which have been supposed to improve eyesight and night vision. They have also been thought of as driving away evil spirits and as benevolent spirits themselves.

There is a practical side to our liking for owls, too. This aspect is discussed, with particular reference to the familiar Barn Owl, later in this chapter.

Turning to the dislike man has often had for owls, we find that only a little of this stems from the fact that owls are predatory birds. Many people, even today, are conditioned so much by their childhood picture of an owl that they are surprised to find the bird is a kind of carnivore. Man tends to have a basic dislike for animals which kill other creatures (though he often conveniently overlooks his own shameful record in this respect, and particularly his record with

Above
A Tawny Owl epitomizes the 'wise old owl', and is regarded with some affection by many. To others it is a killer fit only for persecution.

Left
The ghostly Barn Owl – a familiar owl, tolerated and encouraged, and yet still with an aura of mystery about it.

It is difficult not to think of owls as vaguely man-like!

More young Barn Owls. Farmers have encouraged this bird to breed in their barns and outhouses.

regard to his own species) and when man begins to see an owl in this light he develops a distaste for some of its habits. Man will also dislike owls as killers for other reasons entirely – again, this is an aspect we shall come back to later.

Superstition has probably played a greater part in forming man's attitudes to owls on the debit side. Basically, owls are rather mysterious beings, coming and going by night and hiding themselves away by day – their very association with the darkness and all its terrors and mysteries

in the human mind could hardly make it otherwise. The night is the time when evil is said to be abroad, and when death, too, claims most of its victims, so that there has often been an automatic association of owls with the powers of darkness – and the appearance of eerie-looking Barn Owls and also ghostly sounding Tawny Owls around ruins, old buildings, and churchyards only serves to heighten the illusion. Owls have, therefore, been regarded as birds of ill omen, foretelling misfortune and illness or, at the very worst, death. They have been portrayed as the companions of black magicians and the familiars of witches; and are widely used in literature as birds connected with misfortune.

The whole subject of owls in mythology and superstition is a fascinating one, well worth a book on its own. Here we have only touched on the broad outlines, but the interested reader can find out more about this intriguing area from some of the books listed later.

Turning now to the practical side of man's involvement with owls – the fact rather than the fancy – we must first of all draw a quick sketch of man's own progress from prehistoric times. At the outset, he was essentially a hunter; it was a very long time before he rose from this lowly estate and began to till the land and to keep livestock. Gradually, in various civilizations at various times, man the hunter became man the farmer, and we might hazard a guess that his activities in this sphere began to have some effect on owls, in Europe at any rate, some 4000 years ago when he first began to grow crops on a large scale. Until then, his way of life probably scarcely impinged at all on owls or indeed any other predatory birds.

One of the first things agricultural man began

an increase in the number of small rodents using it as a new source of food, either out in the fields or around man's farms and homesteads where he processed his crops. In turn, this would surely have led to an increase and spread in those predators which eat small rodents – among them the Barn Owl. Other owls too – probably including the versatile Tawny Owl in Europe – no doubt used this new or bigger food source in a more limited way.

The Barn Owl became a common part of the rural scene long ago, moving in to live in close association with man around his farms and homesteads because these provided not only new sources of food but also new kinds of nesting places. Whatever his feelings of superstition about this ghostly white owl, man soon saw the Barn Owl as a most useful ally in his ceaseless fight against rodents – the rats and mice that ate his corn, and other things too. His early observations and opinions, that the Barn Owl did nothing but good by eating his small enemies, have stood the test of time. Modern scientific research has shown that this species is essentially a rodent eater which does no harm at all to man's interests. The result of

A staunch ally on the land, the Barn Owl is a rat killer in a class of its own.

to do was to clear large areas of forest and woodland to make way for his fields with their animals and crops. Undoubtedly, this would have reduced the populations of woodland owls to some extent but it is important to realize that even up to a few hundred years ago there were vastly greater areas of woodland than there are today. Therefore, any reduction in the numbers of woodland owls should not be seen in too drastic a light. On the other hand, we can suppose that the development of agricultural land, particularly where this involved arable land, led to

all this, long before ornithologists came along, was that the Barn Owl was a welcome neighbour, even to the extent that it was provided with basic nesting requirements in some countries and actively encouraged and protected in others. Certainly it was not often molested. It is also reasonable to assume that for many hundreds of years man continued to live in harmony with other owl species, too.

Interestingly, this general state of affairs continues in many parts of the world as far as owls and other birds of prey are concerned wherever

Friend or foe? A
Great Horned Owl
with a Grey Squirrel.
It is not a blood-
thirsty killer but a
predator fulfilling a
useful natural role
in the countryside.

farming remains primitive by Western standards or where man survives as a true hunter in his own right. It is really only when there is a civilization boom of one kind or another that the picture changes. Thus, to a large extent, owl problems have only come about in areas where man has made, or is in the process of making, major changes to his environment.

In the latter half of the 1700s, and through into the 1800s, many new techniques were being discovered which gave rise to the so-called 'agricultural revolution' but it is doubtful whether these new methods affected owls very much, and where changes were occurring it seems likely that owls gradually adjusted to them. From this period onwards, though, a new factor was emerging which was to have far-reaching effects on the countryside, and especially on predatory birds: the rise in field sports and the rearing of game birds. We shall come back to this thorny subject after considering later

changes in agricultural practices which have undoubtedly had quite marked effects on owl populations.

The greatest period of change in agricultural techniques generally, and in the methods of arable farming which concern us here, has been during the last three decades. During this period we have seen full-scale mechanization, the creation of much larger field units, the disappearance of hedges and trees in great numbers and much modernization in farm buildings. All of these changes have removed a certain number of nest sites of the kind used by Barn Owls in particular and, relatively speaking, have in many areas led to a decrease in the numbers of small rodents which were around in former times. As long ago as 1932, a Barn Owl census carried out by the Royal Society for the Protection of Birds had revealed, rather surprisingly, that the national Barn Owl population in Great Britain was as low as 25000 birds, and no doubt the numbers fell still further with changes in farming methods adding their effects to the persecution which was already taking some toll of this species. Barn Owls were probably already becoming rather uncommon birds in some of the most intensively farmed areas of England, such as East Anglia, before the next great scourge of predatory birds came along – toxic chemicals.

By the early 1960s, it was becoming obvious that something drastic was happening to the populations of certain birds of prey, among them the Peregrine Falcon, the Sparrowhawk, the Kestrel, and the Barn Owl – the last two in eastern England especially. In the case of the Peregrine, a study of their population initially carried out as part of an investigation into claims by pigeon fanciers that a large and increasing Peregrine population was wreaking havoc on their birds suddenly revealed that this bird had declined drastically in Britain, and was also having much less breeding success than formerly. At the same time, Sparrowhawks were disappearing from parts of eastern and southern England where they had once been tolerably common, and there were noticeable decreases in the numbers of Kestrels and Barn Owls, too, in these largely agricultural regions. Meanwhile, in Scotland, it was found that Golden Eagles in an area in the west Highlands where sheep farming was a primary form of land use were rearing far fewer young than was normal. In time, similar trends were being detected elsewhere, in the United States and in other parts of Europe.

All of these drastic changes were found to be linked to a new form of environmental pollution caused by the use of certain toxic chemicals in agriculture. A great campaign against their use was instigated as naturalist/scientists, especially in Great Britain and the United States, began to amass more and more evidence about these new dangers, and a horrifying book, *Silent Spring*, by Rachel Carson, brought the whole issue before the public in a most dramatic way.

The substances concerned were a group of chemical pesticides called 'chlorinated hydrocarbons', of which DDT is easily the best known. Others which were to achieve notoriety included dieldrin, aldrin, and heptachlor. In an era when chemical aids to farming were becoming more and more essential to kill harmful insect pests and to help farmers to get bigger and bigger yields of food from the land, these substances came as a boon: they were highly effective and, from the point of view of the job they did for the farmer, a blessing in every way. Unfortunately, little or no thought had been given to the fact that they may have had some harmful side effects. It turned out that they were also deadly to a number of other forms of wildlife which inevitably came into contact with them – they were non-selective killer substances which were doing far more than their originators ever intended. In addition, they were found to be highly persistent, that is, they did not break

down in the soil or as they drained away but remained active, and deadly, for many years after their original application.

Their greatest harmful side effect was on predatory animals, including birds of prey and owls, which are at the top of what is called a food chain. At the bottom of the food chain there is, for example, the grain which is dressed with a substance such as dieldrin to combat the ravages of the wheat-bulb fly. These insect pests are eradicated, or at least decimated, by the chemical but, because of its very persistence, it did not quickly disappear once its job was done. Small rodents feeding on the contaminated grain form the next stage in the food chain, taking large amounts of the chemical into their systems where, again, it remained active and intact. The next and final stage in this particular food chain is formed by the owl or hawk which eats the mammals – themselves perhaps rendered easier to catch through sub-lethal effects of the ingested pesticides. By the time the predator has eaten just a few small rodents, it may have taken into its own system enough chemical residue to cause it to die a horrible death through poisoning. What in some ways seems worse is that the effects of sub-lethal levels of the chemical can cause various physical disorders and infertility. Birds of prey have been found to lay thin-shelled eggs, which break very easily in the nest, to be sufficiently unbalanced to eat their own eggs, or to be so disoriented that they cannot incubate their eggs or give proper attention to breeding matters.

Different birds of prey were affected in different ways by these toxic chemicals, according to their particular food chains and the

The use of certain toxic chemicals as pesticides in agriculture had some disastrous side effects. Many birds of prey died, including numbers of Barn Owls in some regions.

Another victim of
toxic chemical
poisoning – this
time a Tawny Owl.

Luckily, owls do not
seem to have fared
too badly during the
'toxic era' and
species such as the
Barn Owl have only
declined in a few
areas.

substances with which they came into contact. Not only chlorinated hydrocarbons have been involved – the widespread use of mercury compounds in some countries, notably in Scandinavia, has also produced some frighteningly large declines in some populations of raptors and other birds. As far as owls are concerned, though, it seems that those hit hardest have been the rodent hunters of open country and particularly farmland, of which the Barn Owl stands out as the one species which has suffered in particular. There is a good deal of evidence, however, to suggest that the harmful affects of toxic chemicals, while bad enough, have not been quite so drastic among owls as they have with some of the diurnal birds of prey. There is no parallel with the Peregrine, for example, of which the population has only just started to recover from its crash in Britain and which is fast disappearing from a number of European countries and has actually become extinct as a breeding bird in the eastern United States. This is a bird which was, and is, widely persecuted by man and which has been pushed to the brink of extinction by chemical poisoning. Of all the Barn Owls analysed in Britain for chlorinated hydrocarbon residues, only a very few were found to have ingested enough to have caused death. In other countries, including the United States, in areas where conditions of pesticide usage are similar to those obtaining here, no declines in Barn Owl numbers have been detected which could be directly attributed to toxic chemical poisoning.

While this leads to the conclusion that owls have probably escaped the worst ravages of an ecological disaster of considerable magnitude among birds of prey, it should be said that very little work has been done on the effects of sub-lethal doses in owls, which might be expected to be similar to those discovered among other birds of prey. The tremendous outcry which raged for a whole decade in Europe and America, often highly emotional and confused, has fortunately led to enforced or voluntary bans on the use of some of the most harmful substances in many countries. It may be that we have just caught the problem in time. Nevertheless, some of these toxic chemicals are still widely used in some areas, and the efforts of the chemical manufacturers – who, in all fairness to them, were not found to be wanting when they were eventually convinced of the harm being done by some of their products – have not yet managed to replace all the 'super-pesticides' with safe alternatives. Furthermore, we know that much of our environment is heavily contaminated and it is too soon to know what the final effects will be. New pollutants are arising, too, from various substances liberated in industrial waste, and their side effects are only now being revealed. Finally, while Europe and America may have acted in time, some chlorinated hydrocarbons are being used in massive quantities in the developing countries. We have no way of knowing how these substances might be affecting raptor and owl populations there, but it would be surprising if similar situations to those we have known were not already in existence.

The view seems to be general that, with those owl species we know most about, the problem of chemicals is no longer grave, if indeed it ever did have widespread effects on most of them. A much more serious situation, and one which has been with us for much longer, concerns the direct persecution of owls by man, largely in the interests of game preservation.

Even though much research has been carried out among various predatory animals, for many reasons, and even though many of the results have been widely publicized, our ignorance and bigotry is surprising. It has been shown time and time again that there is a basic rule – one we have already noted when looking at owls: predators do not control the numbers of their prey, but vice versa. There are, indeed, some situations where the rule is broken but usually these are the result of man's activities and he has the power to redress the balance, often without the mass slaughter of the predators concerned. To be fair, there are also cases where predator control is justified but these are relatively few. For the most part, however, there is really no need to adopt an attitude which says 'the only good owl is a dead one'; the same applies to other misunderstood creatures such as sharks, crocodiles, and snakes, and birds of prey of all kinds.

If we look at the origins and history of persecution in the British Isles we shall see well enough how raptors and owls there have fared; by changing some dates and places, we could draw a similar picture for a number of other European countries, or draw parallels with situations in parts of the New World – even though the problem is essentially a European one where the preservation of game stocks is concerned.

During the 1800s, hunting for sport grew immensely in popularity. There was a great vogue for shoots, and efforts to provide and protect game increased greatly. The intensive rearing of game birds, for example, became a major operation over wide areas of the countryside. While all this was going on, it was inevitable that attention would be drawn to the fact that certain predators would kill game birds: they had always done so, but now it seemed to matter. Consequently, there began a colossal campaign against 'vermin' – a liberally interpreted expression which included just about every bird and animal which could, or was thought to be able to kill game species. Literally every bird which had a hooked beak automatically went on the 'vermin' list – all the owls included. As the many published game returns show all too clearly, the slaughter which went on through the 1800s and until the time of World War I was immense. Birds of prey of all kinds perished in their millions as gamekeepers shot, trapped, and poisoned them. It sometimes seems

The Eagle Owl is persecuted as vermin throughout Europe, quite unnecessarily, and even shot for sport in some countries.

legal protection to almost all raptors and owls so that we could be forgiven for thinking that the slaughter is now a thing of the past and the problem has disappeared. Unfortunately, this is not the case. Old ways and beliefs die hard, and every year – both openly and surreptitiously – large numbers of raptors and owls are shot, their nests are found and destroyed, they are killed by poison baits, and they are trapped in illegally used, barbaric instruments. The law is flouted, sometimes quite openly, and even when successful prosecutions are brought against those few offenders who are caught, ludicrously small and wholly inadequate fines are often imposed. It is an undoubted fact that those landowners and their 'keepers who still persecute birds of prey are in a minority and that many of their number are wholeheartedly against such things, but the damage done can be enormous.

Owls possibly suffer less from the more direct forms of killing than some of the diurnal raptors, like Sparrowhawks and others, but there are many casualties, especially among the two British woodland owls – the Tawny and Long-eared. Both are also the all-too-frequent victims of a particularly barbaric device known as the pole trap. This is simply a gin trap set on a pole (or a fence post or similar prominent feature). Many hawks and owls like to perch on such places while foraging for prey – with disastrous results. The jaws of the trap snap shut around one or both legs and the thrashing victim is left hanging upside down when the trap falls from its position and is held by a short length of wire or a chain attached to the post. The bird then dies a horrible and often lingering death, clearly in great agony. Quite apart from being both cruel and illegal, pole traps are obviously unselective. Almost any bird apart from an owl or a hawk might be captured, and the author has seen one which, by a particularly cruel twist of irony, held one of the very birds it was set to protect – a Pheasant.

Nobody who has had any dealing with bird protection is under any illusions about how widely these traps are still used. Even while this book was being written, the author was shown one containing a dead cock Blackbird. A few years ago, the Royal Society for the Protection of Birds, determined to bring the whole business into the open, mounted a full-scale campaign against the pole trap. This was greeted by enthusiastic support on the part of many countrymen, 'keepers, and landowners, and with derision by some others who insisted such things either no longer existed or were so few that there was really no need to bother. Enough cases of the deliberate use of pole traps came to light to silence the sceptics for all time and there was a good number of prosecutions; owls were found in plenty as victims. It is still possible to find pole traps in use but perhaps it is not too much to hope that their days are numbered at long last.

Owls continue to be persecuted because they are alleged to do a great deal of damage to game-

miraculous that any survived at all but somehow they did. Others were not so lucky: birds such as the Osprey, wrongly accused of harming fishing interests, were all but exterminated and the collectors of eggs and trophies did the rest. The Goshawk and the Red Kite either disappeared or were left with tiny, relict populations. Owls fared rather better, by virtue of their nocturnal habits, but whenever the chance arose they too would be slaughtered. Whether they were known to be doing any damage or not was immaterial; they were 'vermin'!

World War I afforded a breathing space for birds of prey, while 'keepers were enlisted. There are still old 'keepers about who talk of the great increase in 'vermin' they discovered when they came home. The slaughter resumed, on a somewhat reduced scale, until another war repeated the process all over again.

In the thirty years following World War II, great advances have been made in our knowledge of the ways of predatory birds. It has been shown that they do not usually affect game stocks at all to any serious extent and that the crude term 'vermin' scarcely fits them in any way. Little by little, landowners and their gamekeepers have come to develop a new awareness of the role of birds of prey, owls included, and have left them alone. The passing, in 1954, of the first all-embracing bird protection act gave

Above left
A Tawny Owl in a pole trap. This barbaric instrument, though illegal, is still used by gamekeepers, even though it has been shown over and over again that owls and other birds of prey do not adversely affect game bird numbers.

Above
The Scops Owl is virtually a game bird itself in some southern European lands.

Left
A Screech Owl with a young bird. Fortunately, this and the other North American owls have not suffered the heavy persecution meted out to their cousins in Europe.

The Little Owl was once classed as vermin until vindicated by a scientific enquiry which showed it actually killed large numbers of rodents and insect pests.

rearing interests, especially to the chicks of birds like Pheasants and partridges. If this is indeed happening, then surely some action on the part of the gamekeeper is justified. After all, whether we agree with the killing of birds for sport or not, it cannot be denied that those who rear, for example, young Pheasants for release spend a great deal of time and money doing so. Theirs is regarded as a wholly legitimate activity and as such is entitled to fair consideration. Unfortunately, the whole issue has long been bedevilled by much bad feeling and downright obstructiveness, and not only on the side of the sportsmen. Conservationists have produced just about as much narrow-mindedness in many instances and until fairly recently many of them have been totally opposed to any form of compromise.

The answer to the often sweeping claims made by game interests is to find out the facts of the case in question – is there really a problem? And if there is, is it the fault of predators, or of bad management, or even bad weather?

An interesting case arose in the 1920s and 1930s over the Little Owl in England. This species, while widespread on the Continent, is not native to Britain but was introduced during the latter half of the 1800s since when it has become quite widespread and familiar to many of us. But the cry was raised against it that it was killing large numbers of game chicks and also causing high mortality among domestic chickens. There were many wildly exaggerated reports of this small bird's supposed depredations of some wild bird populations as well as on game birds and poultry. When in 1935 the matter came to a head, and the owl stood to be classed as vermin, the British Trust for Ornithology began an enquiry into its food habits.

For one-and-a-half years, the investigation continued, and nearly 2500 pellets were examined, as well as the gizzards of twenty-eight dead owls and prey remains from no fewer than seventy-six nests. All that came to light were two pellets containing game bird chick remains, plus doubtful evidence from one gizzard and the apparent remains of seven poultry chicks. No reports were had of any serious incidents involving big kills, even though appeals were made for such information to be sent in. Instead, the investigation revealed that the bird was eating huge numbers of earwigs, beetles, and other insects, many of which are regarded as horticultural pests.

The Little Owl, then, was vindicated and indeed was recognized to be an ally of man, as it has been in many other European countries where it has enjoyed legal protection for many years. The difference between the true state of affairs and all the wild allegations which preceded the investigation is quite remarkable, and inevitably we are reminded of similar results when other allegedly harmful birds of prey have been investigated in detail.

Another British owl which has long been accused of doing large amounts of damage is the Tawny Owl which, as we have seen, feeds largely on small mammals but often varies this diet in late summer when the ground cover in woodland becomes rather more difficult to hunt through. This bird is blamed for large-scale predation on young Pheasants in their release pens in woods where they are reared in great numbers. For some time, shooting men and their gamekeepers had grumbled about losses to Tawny Owls and not infrequently took the law into their own hands. On the other hand, many conservationists were adamant that the problem did not exist. Who was right? Or did the truth lie somewhere between the two opposing points of view?

An investigation was clearly called for but this time it was an investigation with a difference. In 1973, an Avian Predators Working Group was set up between shooting and conservation interests and, as a logical next step, it was obvious that a joint investigation was called for. A project was organized by the British Field Sports Society, the Game Conservancy, the Royal Society for the Protection of Birds, and the Gamekeepers' Association of the United Kingdom – the last of which later became part of the Wildfowlers' Association of Great Britain and Ireland. A research biologist, David Lloyd, worked on the problem for two years, carrying out his studies on a large number of estates, especially where there had been reports of avian predation. His findings were in fact published while this book was being written.

No fewer than 154 shoots were visited during the study, on which a grand total of 251049 Pheasant poults were released. The percentage killed by birds of prey, Tawny Owls included, was only 0.9. This compared well with three other studies, which admittedly had not been carried out on areas where predation had been reported, where the figure lay between 0.1 per cent and 0.3 per cent. Taking all this information together, Lloyd estimated that birds of prey killed only about one in every 400 poults released.

As some birds of prey were 'controlled' after they had killed Pheasants, the number of kills could have been higher if no action had been taken but it is thought that the figure would not in any case exceed 2 per cent. Less than one third of the estates sampled complained of losing more than 1 per cent of their released poults to birds of prey and where 'mass kills' of more than ten poults in a night were investigated these were found not to be the work of Tawny Owls, as had been suggested, but more likely the work of predatory mammals such as Foxes, dogs, cats, or Mink. Finally, it should be added that about one third of all Pheasants released die or disappear before the shooting season starts and birds of prey are only responsible for 5 per cent of all known deaths – while mammals kill ten times as many.

With specific regard to Tawny Owls, it was found that they tended to kill more poults released at less than five weeks of age than older ones, that predation was twice as heavy among poults released in late June or July (when Tawny Owls are still feeding young) as in August and September, and predation was also greater when release groups numbered more than 500 young birds.

The study not only showed that predation was much less heavy than had been supposed, but that it was possible to reduce it significantly by releasing poults at about seven or eight weeks of age, by letting them out later in the season, and by releasing them in groups smaller than 500. In addition, many suggestions were put forward showing how the release pens themselves could be made more protective for the poults and more predator-proof. Owl damage can occur but the level is low and can be made lower still with sensible precautions. Where there is a proven case of mass predation there is a last resort in that the law does allow the killing of Tawny Owls where it can be shown that they have caused significant damage.

This imaginative study is not only important because it reveals the true position of the Tawny

Successful attempts
are being made to
reintroduce the
Eagle Owl into some
areas of Europe
where it has been
all but eliminated by
man.

Owl as a predator of young game birds and because it makes so many sensible suggestions as to how predation can be lessened. It shows that sportsmen and conservationists can work together if they are willing to do so, to the benefit of both sides and to the advantage of the birds concerned. Let us hope that the excellent example set here will be repeated with other species in other situations.

Yet another owl which has suffered at the hands of man is the Eurasian Eagle Owl. In spite of food studies which show only too clearly that this big owl does not conflict with man's interests at all, it has been ruthlessly persecuted by sporting interests in many countries for so long that it has declined drastically in many parts of Europe. In some regions it was regarded as fair game for any shooter because it was categorized as 'vermin'. In addition, it has a long history of being used as a decoy. A tethered Eagle Owl will attract a variety of birds down for a mobbing session so that sportsmen can shoot them down by the score. It is sad to reflect that many other birds

of prey, already heavily persecuted at other times, have met their fate when attracted down to captive Eagle Owls.

This fine bird faces other threats, too, more directly associated with the march of civilization than persecution. In many areas, its traditional haunts are no longer the quiet, secluded spots they once were, and the appearance of heavy overhead power lines across valleys where Eagle Owls have nested for centuries has led to many casualties as the birds collide with the wires. But perhaps the tide is turning for the Eagle Owl. Increasingly, it is becoming a protected bird and in some parts of Europe very active protection schemes have been set up to improve its chances of survival. There are even schemes to reintroduce it into areas from which it has vanished, using birds reared in captivity. Some notable successes have been achieved in recent years; in Sweden, for example. Some purists object to the process of reintroducing a bird once it has vanished, but surely where man has used his ingenuity to remove a bird he should not be blamed for using it to redress the balance.

The whole subject of introductions or reintroductions has to be considered very carefully, however. With reintroductions, it is vital that the environment is still able to receive the birds back. There is little point in bringing a lost bird back into a changed set of circumstances where it has no hope of surviving. While there is a number of carefully planned and scientifically controlled experiments in reintroduction being carried out in Europe and the United States, with stocks carefully reared in captivity, there is regrettably also a set of projects with much less to recommend them.

The introduction of a species into an area where it has never occurred naturally is generally to be avoided. In more cases than not, this leads to disaster. The examples of what can go wrong are legion but for our purposes one involving an owl tells the story well enough. Not long ago, the South African race of the Barn Owl, sometimes called the Cape Owl, was introduced into the Seychelles to help reduce the considerable rat populations in the coconut plantations there – an innocuous and probably very useful scheme,

or so it seemed. What actually happened was that this resourceful owl took to catching the local birds instead including the chicks of seabirds specially protected in these unique islands. Thus, from becoming a possibly useful addition to the islands' fauna they quickly became a major pest species themselves, capable of wiping out large sections of bird communities which have never known such a predator and are not equipped to deal with one. It has also been suggested that one of the causes of the rarity of the endemic Seychelles Owl is heavy competition from the alien Barn Owl. Nowadays, the latter is ruthlessly sought out and killed wherever possible.

Mention of introductions and breeding in captivity raises the whole issue of owls as captive birds. Many owls seem to do well in captivity, and certainly people seem to enjoy looking at them. In a few cases, breeding from captive stocks is a useful conservation aid. But are too many wild owls being caught and endangered through the desires of some people to put them on show – and to make money out of them? This

A female Snowy Owl at the Shetland nest site. The rigid protection of these birds has also involved showing them to visitors who come from far and wide to see them.

is a difficult question to answer one way or the other, but what is certain is that large numbers of owls are trapped in some countries, often illegally, and are exported, again sometimes illegally, and often under shocking conditions. Studies carried out so far, indicate that owls, like most other birds, are flown all round the world and that there is a considerable trade in them. These are mostly the commoner species. Many countries are looking into the question of tightening up export and import regulations to control this huge traffic in birds which is currently giving cause for considerable alarm. Not the least disturbing feature is that so many die on their way to their new homes. An RSPB/RSPCA study carried out recently recorded ninety-one owls imported into Britain via Heathrow Airport between 1970 and June 1974, of which 13 per cent were dead on arrival; of 659 in transit, bound for other countries (especially the United States) 14 per cent were dead at Heathrow.

We cannot end our brief look at persecution problems without drawing attention to one more important matter – the hunting of owls themselves for sport. If it seems odd that this should

happen, we need only remember that there is still a number of countries in southern Europe where virtually any bird that flies is fair game. The annual slaughter of birds of prey, especially at migration times, is immense, and owls are by no means immune. Italy and Malta are among the worst offenders and here the small, migratory Scops Owl in particular suffers very heavy casualties. There is a mounting campaign to stop the inhumane slaughter of birds – often including protected birds in the very countries where they are shot – but the way is uphill and paved with many difficulties. As we have said before in another context, old ways die hard.

All owls are fully protected by law in Great Britain, and many other European countries have either full or partial protection for these birds. But having a law and enforcing it are two different matters, and laws regarding protected birds are flouted continually in most southern European countries. It can only be hoped that one day, before it is too late, something more concrete will be done to uphold what are, on paper, suitable pieces of legislation.

In looking at owls in the agricultural landscape, mention was made of the effects on them

144

of changing habitats. The sort of country which is home to many owls is changing in other ways, too. One of these is the disappearance of many areas of native forest and woodland, either so that the land can be used for agriculture or so that it can be replanted with fast-growing, coniferous crops of trees of considerable economic importance.

The total removal of woodland cover is bound to result in the disappearance of some owls. Some of the more versatile species, like the Tawny, Ural, and Barred Owls, have shown that they are able to adjust to some extent by spreading into suburban areas with parks and gardens, where they can modify their food and take more birds than they did before. The Barn Owl, too, has shown an ability to do much the same sort of thing. But there is a number of other owls for which the loss of their habitat spells disaster, and this is especially true of many with isolated populations or a distribution restricted to certain small islands. This is the case with a number of owls in the genus *Otus* – the complex and widespread group which includes many, largely insectivorous species probably beneficial to man's interests. It may not be too extreme to suggest that the disappearance of one or two owls of this sort could result in an insect problem which might then have to be solved by the heavy use of pesticides – with results which might be quite disastrous.

The serried ranks of often alien conifers which form the bulk of forestry plantations have long worried naturalists, especially where they replace old native woodland, as has happened in many regions. While these new woodlands are not without an interest of their own, they often produce a less diverse community of birds and animals and can result in the loss of some 'special' birds altogether. The situation is not quite straightforward, however, because there are stages in the growth of a conifer plantation when it can be distinctly beneficial to some species of birds, and there might even be a case for suggesting that owls often benefit more than some other species.

Young plantations can provide marvellous conditions for big populations of small rodents so that birds like the Short-eared Owl are quick to move into them. For this species at least, then, these plantations can be of considerable value. Later, when the trees grow into taller, denser stands, Long-eared Owls use them readily especially where they adjoin areas of open moorland or the very type of young plantations favoured by their Short-eared cousins. Even the Tawny Owl, ever versatile, will move into coniferous woodland and exist happily where it is not too dense or where there is a good system of rides and clearings.

There is a body of opinion which suggests that having brought wholly alien forests into a country – Sitka and Norway Spruces into Britain, for example – why not introduce some of the birds and animals which live naturally in the same sort of woodland in countries where it occurs naturally? Tengmalm's Owl is one bird which, it is suggested, might fit in quite well. It is certainly a thought, even if commercial spruce plantations bear little comparison to old, natural spruce forest, but for the moment most ornithologists would prefer to see if the indigenous birds can adapt to these new environments (and some are doing quite well as new colonists) before taking such drastic steps.

Agricultural changes and afforestation are, of course, not the only ways in which habitat can disappear. There are also the inexorable spread of towns and cities, the steady expansion of industry, and the ever-increasing network of roads to be taken into account. Every year, large areas of countryside vanish forever under concrete, steel, and tarmac.

Again, some owls adjust while others do not. The basic story is much the same as that we have already told with other kinds of habitat change. Some of the side effects of man's development have interesting results. Airfields, for example, may produce hectares of tarmac and large complexes of buildings, but they can also benefit birds like owls by providing quite large areas of open grassland. These areas often become rich in small rodents and attract Kestrels and Short-eared Owls, in particular, and even Snowy Owls in some areas in North America.

There is a conflict here which can be fatal to owls and humans alike – this is the hazard of the 'bird strike'. It takes only one bird to cause considerable damage to a large, fast-moving plane, sometimes with disastrous results. All manner of bird-scaring techniques have been used to keep runway areas clear, including broadcasting distress calls and using falcons to frighten other birds away. Otherwise, some form of intensive management of the grassed areas is desirable to keep down rodent numbers, but what may solve the problem where owls and hawks are concerned may prove very attractive to large flocks of gulls and other birds!

So far, then, we have seen that the interests of owls and men can conflict in a number of ways, with the owls usually the innocent sufferers. Gradual processes of habitat change are making themselves felt but some owls are able to adapt. In the persecution stakes, there is no adaptation and only man can redress the balance. Nevertheless, owls as an order are clearly a resilient group of birds. We have hinted that some, especially those with a very restricted distribution, may be endangered but, in fact, very few owls are actually in danger of extinction and there is hope for the survival of even the rarest ones. The position is much more precarious among other groups of specialized birds and those which are endemic to certain islands or other small areas. The record of extinction and rapid disappearance among birds like the parrots and rails, for instance, is quite horrifying.

Mauritius is famous – or perhaps notorious would be a better word – for the loss of perhaps the most widely known, extinct bird of all, the

Dodo, a big, flightless bird which was slaughtered by incoming Europeans and vanished forever in a very short space of time. The island has lost two owls too; in the first half of the 1800s, Commerson's Owl disappeared, probably wiped out by man. Little is known about this bird, but it was a large member of the genus *Otus*, a big relative of the scops and screech owls with well-developed ear-tufts. Some remains of a type of barn owl named *Tyto sanzieri* have also been found on Mauritius. Like Mauritius, the nearby island of Rodriguez has lost a number of interesting birds, among them a relative of the Little Owl, named after the island.

Though only one other full species is believed to be lost to us (the Laughing Owl, described later), a number of island races of species which are still extant have disappeared. It seems very likely that the Comoro Scops Owl – a race of the Madagascan species found only on the Comoros – has done so due to human persecution. The Burrowing Owl may still be found fairly easily in some parts of North America, but two of its island races which once lived in the Caribbean region have been extinct since the last years of the 1800s – their disappearance coinciding with the introduction of mongooses. The ground-nesting owls were totally unable to survive the attentions of these alien predators.

The Laughing Owl is probably yet another victim of the introduction of non-native wildlife by man. It, too, is, or was, a ground-nesting owl and it is very likely that its doom was sealed by the introduction to its homeland of stoats, weasels, and cats. The Laughing Owl is a New Zealand bird (called the Whekau by the Maoris) and like a large number of the endemic birds there it has not fared at all well following the coming of the white man, his livestock, and his introduced animals. No doubt rapid changes in land use made a lot of difference too.

The Whekau was a large species of the hawk owl group, usually found only in areas with rocky outcrops along the edges of forest country or in more open terrain. It fed on a wide variety of small animals and birds and is said to have been primarily a rodent eater. It had disappeared from the North Island by the end of the 1800s and was at that time already quite rare on the South Island. Today, some authorities say it still survives in very small numbers in some remote areas, while others, including many New Zealand ornithologists, claim it is extinct. Certainly, it has not been reliably reported in the wild for about forty years. Even so, rumours of its presence still exist and it may yet come to light again, as did the Takahe, another famous 'lost bird' of New Zealand. Even if it does, its future must still be in great jeopardy.

It is interesting to note in passing that New

Malaysian Eagle Owls in captivity. There is increasing concern over the capture of owls for zoos and wildlife parks and over the conditions they endure in transit.

A shameful trade in owls continues unabated in some countries. These Little Owls were among no fewer than 100 offered for sale in an Italian market in 1975.

Zealand's other native owl, the Boobook or Morepork Owl, may be in some trouble in some areas due to competition with a vigorous, introduced species which has existed there now for more than sixty years – the Little Owl. For the moment, though, it is still widespread and, of course, also occurs elsewhere in Australasia.

The Seychelles are another island group where the delicate balance of nature has been upset by man's enterprises and his introduction of aliens. Here we find, if we are very fortunate, the Seychelles Owl, which is currently regarded as a race of the Madagascan Scops Owl but is often treated as a separate species. Today, this very rare bird is found only on the island of Mahé and, indeed, it was long considered to be extinct. After last being recorded in 1906, it was not found when carefully searched for in the 1930s, but it was rediscovered in one small area of mountainous country on Mahé as recently as 1959. Almost nothing is known of the life history of this bird and, like most owls, it is a very difficult bird to census with any real degree of accuracy. In addition, not much is known about the reasons for its decline and great rarity although these may well be linked to disturbance and the loss of its habitat. It has also been suggested, accurately enough in the opinion of some who know the Seychelles well, that the introduced Barn Owl has had a hand in eliminating it by direct competition.

The Madagascar Grass Owl, sometimes called Soumagne's Owl, is a close relative of the barn owls and is found only in parts of Madagascar. It, too, is listed as a rarity and not much is known about its present numbers and distribution. Several more Otus owls are rare or endangered and again these are all birds with a very

limited distribution. The Sokoke Scops Owl, also known as Mrs Morden's Owlet, is a recently discovered bird found only in the remnants of the Sokoke Forest on the Kenyan coast. It is threatened by loss of habitat and also by specimen collectors. Another forest species greatly threatened by the loss of its habitat is the Giant Scops Owl, found only on certain islands in the Philippines. Yet another endangered bird is the Palau Scops Owl, because its lowland mangrove swamp habitat is fast disappearing from the Palau island group in Micronesia. No doubt a number of other island species and races of the Otus owls – and probably others, for example, among the Ninox hawk owls – might also qualify on similar grounds for inclusion in a list of owls which are in danger. But so little is known about many of them that we cannot be sure at the moment.

While it can be seen that most owls are safe, at least for the time being, and only relatively few are in dire straits in survival terms, we should not be complacent about their future as a group: a number of measures remains to be taken.

There is a number of notable exceptions, but for the most part the majority of the world's owls are largely unknown in that hardly any studies have been carried out on their life histories. Nor do we have much more than a vague idea of the numbers of many species, particularly the tropical ones and those with very localized distribution. If we are to take any steps at all towards the better conservation of the world's owls we must first of all devote a considerable amount of energy to studying them in detail. One of the first recommendations we might make to national and international conser-

Nduk Eagle Owl and young – a rare owl with a restricted distribution and one deserving further study. Although it is regarded as a full species by some, it is often treated as a race of Fraser's Eagle Owl, and occurs only in parts of Tanzania.

vation bodies is that they devote some of their resources to this end. There is no denying that the difficulties are immense, especially because owls are often particularly difficult birds to get to grips with and more so because many are confined to such remote areas. But in the long term, research is essential – practical conservation and protection measures flounder when they are not backed up by a good knowledge of the ecological requirements of a species and, of course, there is an initial need for much more survey work to identify which species have problems in the first place.

This is not to say that nothing should be done until we have all the facts at our disposal. Anyone who has been concerned at all with practical conservation will tell you that very often, if you wait too long, it will be too late. There is a number of obviously endangered owls for which the case-history is reasonably well documented and the problems should be tackled right away. Fortunately, steps in the right direction are already being taken in a number of countries to help some owl species.

The preservation of disappearing habitats

through the establishment of nature reserves is all-important to owls that are losing their home-lands. For some of them, it seems that their survival may only be secured if such action is pursued. The snags are legion: difficulties over international relations, conflict over land use and the benefits to people of nature reserves, and, above all, a vast shortage of money to carry out a realistic programme of reserve acquisition. In addition, simple 'protection' on reserves may not be enough. It can work very well with some species but not with others. If a habitat is to be maintained, it cannot simply be fenced in and left to its own devices: it will require management in many cases if it is to remain in its present form. This could be particularly vital in some forest and woodland habitats where they are but relict parts of once greater areas. We come back to research into the birds' ecology, or their relationship to their particular environment and those other creatures which share it with them.

We have already touched on the rather complicated issue of introductions and reintroductions. There is probably no need to introduce

Owls may make fascinating pets but they really belong in the wild.

any owls into areas where they do not or did not occur naturally. Indeed, there are cases on record, as we have seen, where such actions have proved disastrous but bringing back a species into an area from which it has disappeared, or in which its population has reached a low ebb, can be of some help. Some owls breed well in captivity – Eagle and Snowy Owls are notable examples – and carefully regulated captive breeding programmes might well be of great value. As we have said, such notions have to be treated with care but the successes already being achieved with the Eagle Owl in parts of Europe could be emulated with other owls elsewhere.

There is no doubt at all that many owls in temperate regions (and perhaps a few species elsewhere) are being needlessly persecuted by man, usually in the interests of the preservation of game. More research of the kind we have described is very desirable – a thorough knowledge of how owls live and what effects they have on man's activities will go a long way to ·

149

A hand-reared young Tawny Owl. Every summer many are picked up as waifs and taken home by well-meaning people. They are usually within sight of their parents, in fact, and are best left alone or simply moved into cover.

restoring friendly relations between owls and men. Ideally, all owls should be protected by law, as many already are in Europe, North America, and elsewhere. Those involved in conservation and bird protection must not only strive to get laws on to the statute books but must also continue to insist that the authorities enforce these laws – which many do not even in the most conservation-minded countries.

Public opinion could be the owls' greatest ally. It could stop a lot of the persecution which goes on today and effectively outlaw the hunting of owls for fun. It is undoubtedly true that the last few decades have seen an incredible increase in interest in wild creatures and in their preservation. Sometimes, though, the sympathy of the public only goes so far – certain animals and birds are always more 'popular' than others.

Telling people about birds like owls, which kill to eat and may be regarded with some disfavour, must involve telling them about the role of natural predators in nature. In other words, we must convince people that owls (and indeed many other predatory creatures) are not simply attractive to look at – they are wonderful creatures with a highly specialized way of life which form but one part of an intricate mosaic to which we ourselves belong. It should be made apparent that any missing pieces in that mosaic spoil the picture as a whole entity.

In this book, we have glimpsed a number of these fascinating birds and learned a little of how they live. Hopefully, we will also have come to understand them a little better than we did before, and to care about their survival. If this is so, then this book has served its purpose.

The owls of the world

This list follows that given in *Owls of the World, their evolution, structure and ecology*, edited by John A Burton and published by Peter Lowe, which is in itself based on that of JL Peters in Volume IV of his checklist *Birds of the World*, published in 1940, with amendments by later authorities. The classification and nomenclature used in this book follows that of Burton *et al*, to whom the reader is referred for fuller details of the range and distribution of the world's species and subspecies of owls.

ORDER: **STRIGIFORMES**

1 family **Tytonidae** – barn and grass owls
subfamily **Tytoninae**

Tyto soumagnei Madagascar Owl
T. alba Common Barn Owl
T. rosenbergii Celebes Barn Owl
T. inexpectata Minahassa Barn Owl
T. novaehollandiae Masked Owl
T. aurantia New Britain Barn Owl
T. tenebricosa Sooty Owl
T. capensis Common Grass Owl

subfamily **Phodilinae** – bay owls
Phodilus badius Common Bay Owl
P. prigoginei African Bay Owl

2 family **Strigidae**
subfamily **Buboninae** – typical owls
Otus lawrencii Cuban Screech Owl
O. guatemalae Vermiculated Screech Owl
O. nudipes Puerto Rican Screech Owl
O. barbarus Santa Barbara Screech Owl
O. atricapillus Black-capped Screech Owl
O. watsonii Tawny-bellied Screech Owl
O. ingens Rufescent Screech Owl
O. clarkii Bare-shanked Screech Owl
O. albogularis White-throated Screech Owl
O. choliba Choliba Screech Owl
O. roboratus Roborate Screech Owl
O. cooperi Pacific Screech Owl
O. trichopsis Spotted Screech Owl
O. asio Eastern Screech Owl
O. kennicotti Western Screech Owl
O. leucotis White-faced Scops Owl
O. manadensis Celebes Scops Owl
O. podarginus Palau Scops Owl
O. alfredi Flores Scops Owl
O. rutilus Madagascan Scops Owl
O. sunia Oriental Scops Owl

O. scops Common Scops Owl
O. flammeolus Flammulated Owl
O. bakkamoena Collared Scops Owl
O. brookii Rajah's Scops Owl
O. silvicolus Lesser Sunda Scops Owl
O. rufescens Reddish Scops Owl
O. icterorhynchus Sandy Scops Owl
O. ireneae Sokoke Scops Owl
O. spilocephalus Spotted Scops Owl
O. balli Andaman Scops Owl
O. hartlaubi São Thomé Scops Owl
O. sagittatus White-fronted Scops Owl
O. gurneyi Giant Scops Owl

Lophostrix lettii Maned Owl
L. cristata Crested Owl

Bubo virginianus Great Horned Owl
B. bubo Eurasian Eagle Owl
B. capensis Cape Eagle Owl
B. africanus Spotted Eagle Owl
B. poensis Fraser's Eagle Owl
B. nipalensis Forest Eagle Owl
B. sumatrana Malaysian Eagle Owl
B. shelleyi Shelley's Eagle Owl
B. lacteus Milky Eagle Owl
B. coromandus Dusky Eagle Owl
B. leucostictus Akun Eagle Owl
B. philippensis Philippine Eagle Owl

Ketupa blakistoni Blakiston's Fish Owl
K. zeylonensis Brown Fish Owl
K. flavipes Tawny Fish Owl
K. ketupa Malaysian Fish Owl

Scotopelia peli Pel's Fishing Owl
S. ussheri Rufous Fishing Owl
S. bouvieri Vermiculated Fishing Owl

Pulsatrix perspicillata Spectacled Owl
P. koeniswaldiana White-chinned Owl
P. melanota Rusty-barred Owl

Nyctea scandiaca Snowy Owl

Surnia ulula Hawk Owl

Glaucidium passerinum Eurasian Pygmy Owl
G. gnoma Northern Pygmy Owl
G. siju Cuban Pygmy Owl
G. minutissimum Least Pygmy Owl
G. brasilianum Ferruginous Pygmy Owl
G. perlatum Pearl-spotted Owlet

G. *tephronotum* Red-chested Owlet
G. *capense* Barred Owlet
G. *brodiei* Collared Pygmy Owl
G. *radiatum* Barred Jungle Owl
G. *cuculoides* Cuckoo Owlet
G. *sjostedti* Chestnut-backed Owlet

Micrathene whitneyi Elf Owl

Uroglaux dimorpha Papuan Hawk Owl

Ninox rufa Rufous Owl
N. *strenua* Powerful Owl
N. *connivens* Barking Owl
N. *novaeseelandiae* Boobook Owl
N. *scutulata* Oriental Hawk Owl
N. *affinis* Andaman Hawk Owl
N. *superciliaris* Madagascar Hawk Owl
N. *philippensis* Philippine Hawk Owl
N. *perversa* Ochre-bellied Hawk Owl
N. *squamipila* Moluccan Hawk Owl
N. *theomacha* Sooty-backed Hawk Owl
N. *punctulata* Speckled Hawk Owl
N. *meeki* Admiralty Islands Hawk Owl
N. *solomonis* New Ireland Hawk Owl
N. *odiosa* New Britain Hawk Owl
N. *jacquinoti* Solomon Islands Hawk Owl

Sceloglaux albifacies Laughing Owl (*probably extinct*)

Athene noctua Little Owl
A. *brama* Spotted Little Owl
A. *blewitti* Forest Little Owl

Speotyto cunicularia Burrowing Owl

Ciccaba virgata Mottled Owl
C. *nigrolineata* Black and White Owl
C. *huhula* Black-banded Owl
C. *albitarsus* Rufous-banded Owl
C. *woodfordii* African Wood Owl

subfamily **Striginae**
Strix butleri Hume's Tawny Owl
S. *seloputo* Spotted Wood Owl
S. *ocellata* Mottled Wood Owl
S. *leptogrammica* Brown Wood Owl
S. *aluco* Tawny Owl
S. *occidentalis* Spotted Owl
S. *varia* Barred Owl
S. *hylophila* Rusty-barred Owl
S. *rufipes* Rufous-legged Owl
S. *uralensis* Ural Owl
S. *nebulosa* Great Grey Owl

Rhinoptynx clamator Striped Owl

Asio otus Long-eared Owl
A. *stygius* Stygian Owl
A. *madagascariensis* Madagascar Long-eared Owl
A. *flammeus* Short-eared Owl
A. *capensis* African Marsh Owl

Pseudoscops grammicus Jamaican Owl

Nesasio solomonensis Fearful Owl

Aegolius funereus Tengmalm's or Boreal Owl
A. *acadicus* Saw-whet Owl
A. *ridgwayi* Unspotted Saw-whet Owl
A. *harrisii* Buff-fronted Owl

Note 1 In this list, the English name, Hume's Tawny Owl, has been preferred to the Hume's Wood Owl of Burton *et al.*
2 A number of owls sometimes regarded as separate species have subspecies status in this list, that is, *Tyto longimembris* is included with *Tyto capensis*, *Glaucidium jardinii* with *Glaucidium brasilianum*, *Ninox spilonota* and *Ninox spilocephala* with *Ninox philippensis*, *Strix davidi* with *Strix uralensis*, and *Asio abyssinicus* with *Asio otus*.

Further reading

Much of the most detailed work done on owls has been published in ornithological journals, many of which may not be readily available to the general reader. The books listed below are recommended for further reading on owls in general or on certain aspects of their lives. There is now a considerable number of field identification guides and/or regional handbooks covering Europe, Africa, India, parts of Asia, Australia, New Zealand, a few other parts of Australasia, North America, and parts of Central and South America, all of which deal with basic details of owls and their identification: these are not listed here.

Angell, T. 1974. *Owls.* University of Washington Press. Largely personal accounts of North American owls with outstanding illustrations by the author.

Armstrong, EA. 1970. *The Folklore of Birds.* Dover Publications Inc., New York. As its title suggests, a fascinating book. Chapter 7 deals with owls. Originally published in 1958 in the Collins 'New Naturalist' series but now out of print.

Bent, AC. 1961. *Life Histories of North American Birds of Prey: Part 2.* Dover Publications Inc., New York. One of the classics of American ornithology, originally published in 1938 as *Bulletin 170* of the Smithsonian Institution. Includes the North American owls.

Brown LH. 1970. *African Birds of Prey.* Collins, London. Includes a good section on African owls.

Burton, John A (Ed). 1973. *Owls of the World: their evolution, structure and ecology.* Peter Lowe. Written by a team of international experts, very well illustrated, and with the main emphasis on describing all the world's owls. The first standard work on this order.

Craighead, JJ and FCJr. 1969. *Hawks, Owls and Wildlife.* Dover Publications Inc., New York. A classic study of hawks and owls in relation to their prey in Michigan. First published in 1956 by the Stackpole Company and the Wildlife Management Institute.

Grossman, ML and Hamlet, J. 1964. *Birds of Prey of the World.* Clarkson N Potter Inc., New York. A large, detailed book with much information on the world's owls included. Well illustrated.

Geroudet, P. 1965. *Les Rapaces Diurnes et Nocturnes d'Europe.* Delachaux et Niestle, Neuchatel. Perhaps the best and most detailed book on Europe's raptors and owls; in French.

Lloyd, G and D. 1969. *Birds of Prey.* Hamlyn, London. Well-illustrated paperback with a section on the world's owls.

Sparks, J and Soper, T. 1970. *Owls: their natural and unnatural history.* David and Charles, Newton Abbot. A detailed and very readable account of owls and their way of life. Very well illustrated.

Index

154

Acknowledgments

Bruce Coleman Limited: Hans Reinhard front and back jacket.

Colour
Ardea Photographics: Hans Beste 76, 77, KJ Carlson 83 bottom, Werner Curth 67 top,
S Roberts 83 top, 84 top, 84 bottom, John S Wightman 89; Bruce Coleman Limited: John A
Burton 124, Russ Kinne 33, Leonard Lee Rue III 67 bottom, Hans Reinhard 18, James Simon
24; Grahame Dangerfield 115, André Fattras 120; Urpo Hayrinen 32 top, Olle Hedvall 72, 118;
John Hillelson Agency: Shelly Grossman 30, 65 top, 91, 106 top; Eric Hosking 109; Jacana:
F Bell and C Vienne 73, MC Noailles 37, JF & M Terasse 67 bottom, Jacques Vieillard 127;
Frank W Lane: Ronald Austing 36, 105 bottom; Ken Lilly 27; James T McKeen 39;
H Mickelsson 101, 121; Natural History Photographic Agency: Stephen Dalton 125, Peter
Johnson 25, 103; Klaus Paysan 21; Photo Library Inc: Roy Pinney 32 bottom; GW Robinson 20.

Black and white
Aquila Photographics 14, 70, 107 bottom, 133; Ardea Photographics: Hans Beste 100 top left,
KJ Carlson 140, KW Fink 19, Don Hadden 41 bottom right, Edgar T Jones 112, Gary R Jones
98, Peter Steyn 41 bottom left, 46, JE Swedberg 12, 59 bottom, Richard Vaughan 126, Tom
Willock 48; Rudolf G Carlson 47; Bruce Coleman Limited: Des Bartlett 100 bottom, Jane
Burton 111 bottom, Jack Dermid 49, 51 top, MPL Fogden 108 bottom, Cyril Laubscher 55,
Jan Lindblad 75 bottom, Hugh Maynard 78 top right, Graham Pizzey 17 top, Goetz D Plage
29 bottom, Hans Reinhard 17, Gerald Cubitt 29 top; C Everett 28; Olle Hedvall 40, 100 top
right, 101, 113; Eric Hosking 15, 22, 23, 44 left, 66 bottom, 79, 86, 114, 123 top, 136 bottom,
143; Eric Hosking: MS Wood 108 top; Jacana: Arthus-Bertrand 59 top right, Pierre Dupont
64, Frédéric 146; Frank W Lane: Ronald Austing front endpaper, 45, 54, 57, 58 top, 58 bottom,
71, 75 top, 80, 86 bottom, 89, 110 bottom, 111 top, 119 top, 128, 139 bottom, back endpaper,
Lynwood M Chace 61, 66 top, Dan Habecker 69, GE Kirkpatrick 31, 38, 99, Frank W Lane
42 top, 44 right, Georg Nystrand 116, Len Robinson 17 bottom, H Schrempp 139 top right,
KHC Taylor 107 top, Ronald Thompson title page, 88 top, 104 bottom; Richard T Mills 105
right: CK Mylne 68; Natural History Photographic Agency: Andrew M Anderson 81, 104 top
left, DN Dalton 53, 132 bottom, Stephen Dalton 56, 74 top, 130 top, 130 bottom, 149;
Naturfoto: Kaj Boldt 123 bottom, Arthur Christiansen 110 top left, 110 top right, B and H
Frederiksen 93 left, Emil Lütken 78 top left, Ib Trap-Lind 104 top right; Naturfotografernas
Bildbyrå: Edgard Eriksson 13, Björn-Eyvind Swahn 122, Göran Hansson 105 left, Olle Hedvall
88 bottom, 92, 102, Ingmar Holmåsen 51 bottom, 74 bottom, Janos Jurka 87, Peter Lindberg 78
bottom, 93 right, 142, Bertil Pettersson 129, RSPB 136 top, 139 top left, 150; Jaap Taapken 147;
Topham/Coleman 26, 42 bottom, 43, 59 top left, 60, 62, 83, 119 bottom, 116–7, 132 bottom,
134, 135, 138, 144; Zoological Society of London 34, 35, 41 top, 52, 148.

The publishers have made every attempt to contact the owners of the photographs appearing
in this book. In the few instances where they have been unsuccessful, they invite the
copyright holders to contact them direct.